Transference and Transcendence

Transference and Transcendence:
Ernest Becker's Contribution to Psychotherapy

Daniel Liechty

JASON ARONSON INC.
Northvale, New Jersey
London

The author gratefully acknowledges permission to reprint material from *The Denial of Death*, by Ernest Becker. Copyright © 1973 by The Free Press. Reprinted with the permission of The Free Press, a Division of Simon & Schuster.

Production Editor: Elaine Lindenblatt

This book was set in 10 point Bookman by TechType of Upper Saddle River, New Jersey, and printed and bound by Haddon Craftsmen of Scranton, Pennsylvania.

Library of Congress Cataloging-in-Publication Data

Liechty, Daniel, 1954–
    Transference and transcendence / by Daniel Liechty.
        p. cm.
    Includes bibliographical references and index.
    ISBN 1-56821-434-0
    1. Transference (Psychology)   I. Title.
    [DNLM: 1. Becker Ernest.   2. Psychoanalytic Theory.
    3. Psychoanalytic Therapy.   WM 62 L718t   1995]
    RC489.T73L54   1995
    154.2′4—dc20
    DNLM/DLC
    for Library of Congress   94-39365

Manufactured in the United States of America. Jason Aronson Inc. offers books and cassettes. For information and catalog write to Jason Aronson Inc., 230 Livingston Street, Northvale, New Jersey 07647.

Contents

Preface

In the course of completing four graduate degrees, I have read hundreds and hundreds of books. Some were a waste of time. Most were of some value and a small number were excellent. But only three books stand out in my mind as having given me a proverbial kick in the head—books that left me stunned and gasping for breath! The first of these was a novel, *The Last Temptation of Christ*, by Nikos Kazantzakis. The second was a book of academic theology, *The Crucified God*, by Jürgen Moltmann. And the third was Ernest Becker's book, *The Denial of Death*.

I first was introduced to the writings of Ernest Becker in a seminary course on biblical apocalyptic. *The Denial of Death* was part of the assigned reading. I was overwhelmed by the brilliance of this book and proceeded to read everything I could find by Becker. Becker had only recently died and I mourned the loss with each new page.

For me his work has been more than intellectually challenging. In a world of narrow disciplinary specialization, Becker was one of the very few intellectuals who constantly had an eye for the big picture. Closely digesting his work has been a primary stimulation for my own quest for personal growth and self-understanding. More than any other source, Becker has always pointed me toward the right questions to ask. Participating deeply in Becker's own wrestling with what it means to be human has been as valuable to me as psychotherapy. During the past 15 years, I have returned to his books again and again, each time finding something new and fresh that had direct relevance to the changing circumstances in my personal life.

For most of those years I read Becker as a theologian, and his influence, specifically his view of the nature of human evil, is clearly reflected in my book *Theology in Postliberal Perspective* (1990). About the time that book was published, I began clinical work in the mental health field. As I confronted mental illness on a daily basis, I again found myself returning to Becker's writings, not only for insights into the patients but also for help in understanding my own reactions, resistances, and internal emotional transformations, which were brought on by my work.

Becker was a social scientist and not a clinical therapist. He always kept one eye on the usefulness of any particular theory for transformation of society as a whole. His main search was for a serviceable social theory. My concern in presenting Becker's ideas here has been to focus on what might be useful for those in the helping professions. Therefore, I am not presenting a definitive account of Becker's work but rather an exploration and an interpretation.

As with the work of most thinkers, the development of Becker's thought does not progress in a simple linear direction. I have found it more useful to conceive of its development on the model of a conch-like spiral. The same core issues of human behavior and motivation remained throughout the corpus of his work. Each time he returned to a particular problem, he incorporated what he had written before and expanded it with new readings, new metaphors, and new angles drawn from a wide sweep of materials from various disciplines. Therefore, for example, while he began by referring to "low self-esteem," which in later writings became "behavioral poverty," then "alienation," then "sin," and finally "death denial," he was speaking of the same human problem and simply using the language of his current interlocutors to express it. Even his first book, a published form of his Ph.D. dissertation comparing Zen, Chinese thought reform, and psychoanalysis, contains within it the core ideas of an expanded understanding of the phenomenon of transference, which was most important to Becker's work as a whole. Firmly grounded in an empirical, post-positivistic, and pragmatic methodology, as well as an arms-opened embrace of a humanistic identity for social theorizing, Becker's style is what Saleeby (1988) has called "generative" theory as opposed to "normative" theory.

This character of Becker's work makes the format for presenting his ideas in a systematic fashion somewhat arbitrary. A manuscript is read linearly, regardless of the subject material (with the exception, perhaps, of the Talmud). One could present Becker's work by beginning with any number of his ideas and concepts and then continuing to elaborate on them until you have brought in the rest of his work. I chose to take the development of the individual, from infancy through adulthood, as the model for my presentation, looking at personality dynamics from Becker's perspective during the successive phases of life. I am happy with this course of presentation, but would like to make clear to the reader that this is a structure imposed on Becker's writings. It is not contained within the writings themselves. I have thought about this for many hours to discover if, and in what ways, this structural imposition distorts Becker's views. I have no doubt that it does distort them. But since it is my way of having incorporated the material, I remain blind to the distortions, which will have to be pointed out by other interpreters of Becker's work.

Chapter 1 contains a biographical sketch, a brief presentation of his educational theories, and an overview of his "Science of Man," which stem from earlier writings. Although he did not repudiate these early projects, he did neglect them in his later work. It was not that these early projects were wrongheaded. But he came to realize that they had no chance of success in the current social climate, and so he simply let them drop.

Chapter 2 examines Becker's views concerning the primary development of personality dynamics. The reader may recognize there the broad influence of Otto Rank and his revision of the origins of anxiety away from the Freudian sexual theory and back to the earliest maternal/parental merger and separation. Chapter 3 then carries this early learning into the formation of adult character. Chapter 4 takes a closer look at the dynamics of transference. This leads directly into Chapter 5, which suggests that there are very real limitations on what can be accomplished in psychotherapy. Becker was, to put it mildly, anti-utopian in his understanding of mental illness and its treatment. In Chapter 6 I present Becker's views concerning mature, adult psychodynamics. And finally, in

Chapter 7, I suggest some possible directions for therapists.

Ernest Becker's writings are not widely read in the
counseling field, although a few influential figures, most
notably Irving Yalom and Robert J. Lifton, are generous in
their praise of his work. In becoming acquainted with
many different approaches to therapy, I am often left
unsatisfied by the theoretical foundations of many of the
systems that are presented. Especially in those who
trumpet loudly a move "beyond" Freud, I often find that
there is no real substructural view of the human being
involved. What I find instead are a few catchy metaphors
and perhaps some useful therapy techniques. But without
a well-rounded view of the human being on which to base
these metaphors and techniques, I have been left intellectually unsatisfied. Even if such metaphors and techniques
prove useful in therapy, I still feel left up in the air. I want
to know not just that something proves therapeutically
useful, but also how and why, and just what is being
communicated during the therapy session. Freudian theory, even if its interpretations can feel somewhat forced
and its preferred techniques somewhat stiff, at least has
the advantage of being based on a thoroughly fundamental
understanding of human nature and human behavior.

In my view, Ernest Becker has presented an understanding of human nature and human behavior as thoroughly satisfying intellectually as Freudian theory. By
using Becker's views as a base, I have found that many of
the metaphors and techniques offered in various approaches to therapy begin to make sense, that one has a
handle on what is happening during the process of therapy, and that very good insight concerning a proper course
of therapy is produced.

Becker did not write clinical material. He relied exclusively on secondary sources for the case histories that he used to illustrate his ideas. Becker wrote works of academic philosophical anthropology, which is perhaps why clinicians remain only vaguely aware of his insights. Because I have found his work to be so valuable, it is my hope that as a result of reading this book an increasing number of clinicians will also investigate his writings.

It is not my intention to idealize the man beyond his due. My feelings have been well expressed by Robert J. Lifton in a review of Becker's last book, which appeared in the December 14, 1975 issue of *The New York Review of Books*. There Lifton wrote, "I have heard complaints that Becker is wildly associative, dramatically existential, enthusiastic about his ideas to the point of repetition, and less than systematic. Probably so . . . But the power of the work prevails. I salute the legacy and wish I had known the man."

1

Introduction

*We wait
for a fate that never arrives,
a faith that remains unfulfilled.*

S. J. Marks

A LIFE SKETCH

What makes people act the way they do? This was the absorbing question of Ernest Becker's intellectual life. He was determined to pursue this question wherever it led him. Because he refused to allow his search to be confined to the boundaries of any one discipline, his academic career, cut short by cancer, was scattered and stormy. From the time he completed his Ph.D. in 1960 until his death in 1974, he produced a steady stream of books and journal articles of rare and unusual depth in which he outlined his "Science of Man." His works brim with insights for therapists.

Becker was born into a Jewish family in Massachusetts in September 1924 (Leifer 1976). After completing military service, in which he served in the infantry and helped to liberate a Nazi concentration camp, he attended Syracuse University in New York. Upon graduation he joined the United States Embassy in Paris as an administrative officer. Although he valued the experience of living in Paris, he became bored with this work and the prospects of life in the diplomatic corps. Therefore, in his early thirties, he returned to Syracuse University to pursue graduate studies in cultural anthropology. He was attracted to this field because of its interdisciplinary and cross-cultural approach to the study of human beings. His interest soon centered on philosophical anthropology and this remained his consuming passion. Although a simplification, it is useful to think of his intellectual career as a quest to come to terms with what is enduring in the philosophical anthropology of Freud and Marx.

At Syracuse, Becker studied under the Japanese specialist Douglas Haring. He wrote a Ph.D. dissertation that examined the mechanisms of transference in Japanese Zen, Chinese thought reform, and Western psychotherapy. The published version of this work, *Zen: A Rational Critique* (1961a), was dedicated to Douglas Haring. Obviously Becker valued Haring's teaching style and intellectual influence greatly.

After completing his Ph.D., Becker was hired to teach anthropology in the Department of Psychiatry at the Upstate Medical Center in Syracuse. There Becker developed a relationship with psychiatrist Thomas Szasz. Szasz was already making known his criticism of the medical model of psychiatry and the authoritarianism inherent in that model. He had published *The Myth of Mental Illness* in 1961 and this was followed in 1963 by *Law, Liberty and Psychiatry*. Both of these volumes reflect very directly Szasz's unconventional views on mental illness. Because of his own antiauthoritarian leanings, Becker was drawn to the Szasz circle and regularly participated in their discussion group. At the same time, Becker took part in various lectures and symposia at the school and became acquainted with the clinical aspects of psychiatry from the inside.

During this time, Becker published several articles in psychiatric journals, advocating a transactional view of mental illness. He also published two more books that reflected his lectures to psychiatric interns at the center. In both of these books, *The Birth and Death of Meaning* (1962e) and *The Revolution in Psychiatry* (1964b), Becker argued for a broadly transactional understanding of mental illness that was in direct conflict with the medical model. Although these books demonstrate a wide scholarly knowledge of various social science disciplines, they were by no means universally appreciated within the field of psychiatry.

The views of Szasz were rightly understood as a direct attack on current practices in psychiatry and thus he became embroiled in conflict with some entrenched interests within the field. This was especially heated because the works of Szasz and his circle were being used to publicly criticize the practice of involuntary commitment of mental patients. In November 1962, Szasz was disciplined by the New York State Department of Mental Hygiene and was effectively stripped of his teaching duties within the state medical school. This produced a division within the Department of Psychiatry between those who supported Szasz and those who did not. Although Becker had his differences with the political libertarian Szasz, he viewed the censoring as an encroachment on academic freedom and supported Szasz. This was a brave move for an untenured instructor within the department and Becker paid for it dearly. Along with several others, Becker was dismissed from the school. Becker left for a year of writing and reflection in Italy. He would spend the rest of the decade as a gypsy scholar, moving from job to job and department to department nearly every academic year.

Following a year in Rome, Becker returned to spend the 1964 academic year at Syracuse University, not, however, at the medical school but in the education and sociology departments. By this time, the student movements that would characterize the late 1960s were being felt at Syracuse.

Becker never simply identified himself with the youth and was suspicious of the later Dionysian excesses associated with psychedelic drug taking. However, he was openly in favor of the civil rights movement, was against the war in Vietnam, and was very critical of many of the same authoritarian educational practices as were the students. He was vocal especially about the dangers to academic independence and freedom posed by the common practice of the universities to seek and rely on military and business sources for research contracts. This struck at the heart of the financial side of science research and Becker's contract at Syracuse was terminated after one year.

In 1965 Becker moved to the sociology department at the University of California at Berkeley on a similar one-year contract. The following year he received another one-year contract at the same school in the anthropology department. Becker was an innovative teacher and his lectures were always crowded by hundreds of students. Becker's teaching reflected his way of thinking. It was broadly interdisciplinary, and he was eager to apply theoretical formulations to current problems of concern. He was also very theatrical. To illustrate a theoretical point on existential human choice and its relation to madness, Becker drew on Shakespeare's *King Lear*. More than that, however, Becker came to the lecture dressed for the part and used props and stage lighting to deliver his Lear!

The very aspects of Becker's thought and teaching that roused the excitement of intellectual adventure and discovery among his students did not necessarily endear him to other members of the faculty. His willingness to employ literary sources and even theological sources, coupled with his constant criticism of narrowly empirical approaches to social science research, led some academicians to criticize Becker as soft and unscientific. Berkeley did not renew his contract.

The students, however, let their voices be heard in the matter. More than 2,000 students signed a petition demanding that Becker be retained. When this failed, they voted to have his salary as a visiting scholar paid from student funds. The administration expressed willingness to use these funds to have Becker remain as an educational consultant, but were unwilling to allow students to hire their own professors. (This incident is reported in the news article "A Class Hires a Scholar" in the March 10, 1967 issue of *Time* Magazine.) Becker's courses, under this arrangement, would be noncredit. Becker decided to take an offer to teach social psychology at San Francisco State University, which was a step down from Berkeley. Yet Becker had high hopes for this institution. Its president, S. I. Hayakawa, was one of the key originators of the interdisciplinary science of general semantics. Surely at an institution under his leadership, a broad generalist social scientist like Becker could expect a supportive administration. Unfortunately, it was not to be. For in the very year (1967–68) that Becker joined the faculty, the student revolts literally erupted like a volcano on that campus. Hayakawa, supported by Governor Ronald Reagan, called in the National Guard to maintain order. Becker did not feel he could teach freedom with armed police outside of the lecture hall.

In 1969, he resigned from his position and moved to Simon Fraser University in Vancouver. There he joined an interdisciplinary department that combined sociology, anthropology, and political science. This was the ideal place for a man like Ernest Becker. It was there that he not only published a thoroughly revised edition of *The Birth and Death of Meaning* (1972) but also wrote his masterpiece, *The Denial of Death* (1973), its sequel, *Escape from Evil* (1975), as well as a remarkable essay on loneliness (1974c). *The Denial of Death* was awarded a Pulitzer Prize in the category of nonfiction. His last work, as it would turn out, was published posthumously. For in late 1972, Becker was diagnosed as having stomach cancer. He died, at the age of 49, in March 1974 (Keen 1974).

CULTURAL PLURALISM AND POSTMODERN PSYCHOTHERAPY

Psychology has assumed that there is behavior that can be identified as normal and behavior that deviates from this norm. Psychology found its roots in attempting to establish the laws of normal development, which leads to normal behavior, and through this to gain understanding of abnormal behavior. Although tolerance and a nonjudgmental attitude have been held in high regard for the practice of psychotherapy, it has been essential to the discipline to identify disorders in behavior and personality development. Therapy itself aims at moving the client or patient toward normal behavior. This is the classical paradigm for intrapsychic psychotherapeutic practice.

Recently psychotherapists and counselors, especially those who are really front-line workers in the delivery of psychotherapeutic services, have been raising serious questions concerning this paradigm (Gergen 1990, Gorman 1993, Jager 1991, Kitwood 1990, Kvale 1990, Mailick 1991, Roffey 1993, Saleeby 1994, Shotter 1990). Practitioners are becoming increasingly aware of the role that culture plays in shaping assumptions about normal behavior. Inheritors of the psychotherapeutic tradition, these practitioners are recognizing that narrowly intrapsychic models are inadequate.

In modern cities today, what might be considered normal or deviant behavior can change from neighborhood to neighborhood. For those living in environments of extreme pluralism, that which in the classical paradigm could be assumed as normal comes to be seen as itself a social and cultural construction. With no final court of appeal to decree what normal behavior is, practice within contexts of extreme cross-cultural pluralism has radically revised or even jettisoned much of the theory on which psychotherapy was based.

The living situation of extreme cross-cultural pluralism is the social context for a new way of thinking, a move from modernism to postmodernism. The postmodern turn has been identified in all of the human sciences. It is a many-faceted phenomenon and has had differing consequences in various disciplines. Science has traditionally privileged the position of the detached rational observer in research and epistemology. But because even the most sensitive and self-examined observer carries his or her own cultural norms as an integral part of the process of living, it is exactly this detached rational position that postmodernism has brought into question. Postmodernism is a move away from detached theory toward that of the participant observer engaged in a two-way process of learning (Rorty 1979).

The dominant theme in postmodernism is what Gergen (1990) has called a thoroughgoing perspectivism. This is another way of speaking about the context of pluralism. The observer is bound to his or her particular perspective, which itself is the by-product of language and social interchange, that is, of communication and relationship. Knowledge derives from communicative interaction, which in turn dictates the parameters of conceptualization. What in a given social context is recognized as reality is not simply a reflection of what is objectively there, but is an interpretation mediated through the communicative process. Viewed in this light, the use of language is the most powerful force of social control. Contrary to the child's rhyme "sticks and stones . . . ," as Hartman (1991) states, "words create worlds."

Although the postmodern transition was first articulated in the late 1970s, a number of important postmodern themes are found in Ernest Becker's earliest writings, for example, in his presentation of mental vulnerabilities such as depression in terms of socialization, gaming, and "language competence" (Becker 1961b, 1962b,c,d, 1974b, 1990).

Becker suggested that because the ego is rooted in social reality, a comprehensive understanding of mental vulnerabilities such as depression must extend beyond the intrapsychic to the entire range of social phenomena. Drawing on the work of Szasz (1961) and Goffman (1959), Becker viewed social interaction in terms of games. Each type of interaction has its own rules, or grammar, which maintains the significance of the interaction. Games of social interaction are staged dramas in which the person, the social performer, is provided with rituals to enhance self-esteem. Meaningful actions are those actions that serve to enhance self-esteem. But self-esteem is itself a symbolic linguistic construction. It is the person's ability to view his or her actions within a narrative that makes sense. Therefore, a hermeneutical circle is formed by self-esteem, games (i.e., communication and relationship), and meaningful narrative.

In Becker's formulation, it is language that commands attention in meaningful action and spurs one on to further action. It is language that makes action meaningful for human beings, because of our need for symbolic cohesiveness. Words, in short, are how we maintain a sense of continuity in identity.

> We are paralyzed to act unless there is a verbal prescription for the situation. Non-verbal situations do not commit our attention and hence do not call up action. . . . when action bogs down, meaning dies. For man, it suffices that verbal action bogs down in order for meaning to die. . . . if the individual can keep verbal referents going in a consistent scheme, action remains possible and life retains its meaning. [Becker 1962b, p. 31]

Becker viewed such vulnerabilities as depressive self-accusation and paranoid fantasies as attempts to keep the verbal action going and to place events in some kind of narrative of meaning. That there is truly no meaning in life is the one thing that human beings simply cannot face, and without some narrative of meaning, as logotherapy has reminded us, life is not possible. Even attempts by philosophers and others to assert that life has no final or metaphysical meaning are placed within some smaller

narrative of meaning. The person with depressive or paranoid vulnerabilities would rather see oneself as at fault or
the target of evil than to have no narrative of meaning at
all.

Becker suggested further that this hermeneutical
circle applied to societies and cultures as well as to the
individual. The narrative of meaning for an individual
might center on family, career, religious belief, and the
like. The narrative of meaning for a nation might have to
do with its monarchy, its constitutional government, or its
economic system. The narrative of meaning for an entire
culture might be centered on advancing civilization or
some other of what Lyotard (1984) called the "grand
narrative." For the individual, mental vulnerabilities such
as depression occur when there is a break in that person's
hermeneutic circle—for example, following the death of
one who was central to that person's games and narrative.
Likewise, sociologists and anthropologists have identified
a condition they call *anomie,* which may occur in a nation
or culture after an event that places the taken-for-granted
truth of its grand narrative into grave doubt—for example,
when an isolated culture is suddenly intruded upon by
more powerful outsiders.

It is not my intention here to suggest that Becker was
the first postmodernist social thinker, nor even that he was
steadfastly consistent in his views on the nature of mental
illness, although he did reiterate what he called an "anti-
idealist" view of communications in one of his final essays
(Becker 1974b). The relative worth of Becker's work does
not rise or fall with how well he can be made to fit the
current intellectual paradigm. But it is worthy of note that
Becker was most in touch with postmodernist themes in
exactly those areas where the postmodern position inter-
sects with clinical practice (Saleeby 1994). Perusal of his

early essays might be a more readily comprehensible way into a postmodern understanding of mental health than slogging through the often obscure prose of self-consciously postmodern theorists. Furthermore, I suggest that in following Becker's work through to the concept of denial of death, therapists and counselors will find one avenue forward within the postmodernist paradigm, rather than only the nihilistic dead ends that have been the consequences of some postmodernist approaches.

HUMAN EVOLUTIONARY ADVANCEMENT

As part of the evolutionary genesis of species, human beings share the physical and even emotional traits of their animal cousins. However, human behavior is in specific areas quite different from other primate behavior. It is the uniqueness of human behavior that intrigued and fascinated Becker. Drawing on a broad range of investigations and writings, Becker pointed toward human language as that which qualitatively sets human thought and behavior apart from other primate behavior.

We do not have concrete knowledge of when language developed among that peculiar ape species from which human beings have descended. Nor are we able to adjudicate decisively between the various theories for how this development took place. But we are sure of the fact that with the development of language, human self-consciousness was made possible, replacing instinctual stimulus-response behavior. This is what is, in essence, distinctive about human behavior and human existence.

Becker meditated at length on this development (Becker 1962e). He repeatedly suggested, in a way that somewhat reifies the evolutionary process, that this development of individual self-consciousness in one species is a great experimental leap forward by the evolutionary process itself. This development of self-consciousness in one species Becker presented as the first really great revolution in evolution—that is, where something qualitatively new came into existence (Becker 1968a).

The grand narrative our culture tells of the human species describes a steady outworking of this great evolutionary experiment in self-consciousness, an experiment that gave to human beings the real possibility of rising above the constrictions of nature itself. But this very gift of human subjectivity contained within it its own special constrictions. While the development of language and symbolic expression allowed for conscious cooperative efforts among human beings far beyond that of any other species, this also created in human beings a peculiar kind of socialization into group behavior.

The subjectivity and sense of self that each individual achieves is dictated directly by the cultural symbol system into which that individual is born (Becker 1962e). Each person gains a sense of well-being by automatic and uncritical performance within that cultural symbol system. In short, by our upbringing and entrance into the social environment, we are symbolically reinstinctivized within a particular worldview (Becker 1968a). The individual sense of self, of nature, of morality, are all imparted in a reflexive and uncritical manner by the human environment. It is as if the evolutionary process raised the human individual up from the other animals, only to quickly and quietly tuck him right back down again, as solidly and firmly as before.

But the complete story is not yet told. By critically examining human behavior, human beings have been able to discover the mechanisms by which they have been symbolically reinstinctivized. This, in Becker's view, is the radical importance of Freud's psychoanalytic idea of the Oedipus complex. Although Becker was critical of Freud's narrowly sexual interpretation of the concept, he saw the elucidation of the Oedipus complex as one of the major achievements of Freud and psychoanalysis.

Becker understood the Oedipus complex as a kind of shorthand expression for the early conditioning process that each child undergoes (Becker 1962e). It is the mechanism by which the child gains a cultural worldview, a sense of self-worth, and a sense of morality. But because this is imparted to the child before the child has any idea of what is happening and at a time when the child is in an overwhelmingly inferior position in relation to his or her environment, the resulting sense of self and of the world is bought at the price of independent thought and action. The child must gain a sense of power vicariously from others. Rather than becoming truly powerful and independent the individual is tied emotionally to whatever model of power was presented during the conditioning process.

As Becker saw it, the human species stands on the edge of a possible major revolution in the evolutionary process. Freud made this mechanism of reinstinctivization known to us. It is now an object for our conscious reflection and no longer something buried deep within the gulf of the unconscious mind. Having become an object for conscious reflection, it is at least thinkable that the process could be somewhat altered, opening up completely new possibilities for human freedom.

In Becker's view, the lion's share of the evil that forms the narrative of human history stems directly from the unconscious and uncritical allegiance to the symbolic meaning systems that the various cultures and societies have developed. Human beings gain their sense of safety and worth by blindly following the internalized modes of power and authority that were presented by the parents, family, social group, and nation during the socialization process. Rather than becoming a center of thoughtful free choice, the individual fights to protect those internalized models of power on which his life has come to depend (Becker 1973).

Helping individuals gain understanding of what they have uncritically accepted during the socialization process, thereby allowing for at least the possibility of renewal and change, is essentially an educational job. It is the task of psychoanalysis at its best. But psychoanalysis is too time-consuming and too easily derailed to be the basis for a social movement or for species transcendence. In Becker's view, that is the task of public education. This forms the background for his philosophy of education.

EDUCATIONAL PHILOSOPHY

Becker presented his philosophy of education in a chapter contribution entitled "Personality Development in the Modern World: Beyond Freud and Marx" (1963) and in his book *Beyond Alienation: A Philosophy of Education for the Crisis of Democracy* (1967). Becker protested against the overly departmentalized system of education found especially in the major research universities. He saw this as a direct effect of each discipline seeking to maintain and extend its own power within the system. It was not a result of studied attempts to enhance the education of students. An overall and integrated approach to knowledge had been sacrificed because of this strict separation between departments and disciplines. Lacking a centering focus for education, teachers and researchers in each discipline continue to plod along, churning out ever narrower research results, but with no opportunities to integrate knowledge and aid in the progress of society at large. Becker suggested that the focus for an integrated and synthetic approach to education would be the concept of alienation.

Becker aimed to provide through this integrated approach to education a unified and critical worldview from which people could work to solve the basic problems of human adaptation in a changing social environment (Becker 1967). Understanding that it is difficult to arrive at agreement on desired political and social problems in the abstract, Becker suggested that the problem be approached from the other side. That is, agreement could be reached on what is *undesirable* for human life. That would be the working definition of alienation. Alienation works against the fullest promotion of human freedom and the fullest possible development of human talents.

Each discipline would have its contribution to make to a general theory of alienation. A general theory of alienation would elucidate how the freedom and responsible choice of each person is constricted by the man-made arrangements of society. It does not have to define the good in terms of results, for society is constantly changing and we cannot know in advance what the good will be. By explaining what is not good, by teaching students to recognize the causes of alienation, direction is given to education that would best allow people to adapt to changing social conditions.

While at Syracuse, Becker tried to gather together an informal group of academics representing as wide a disciplinary spectrum as possible for discussion of this integrated curriculum. He could find very few who were willing to participate. The most steadfast of these was the Protestant chaplain of the university (Becker 1977). Although the vision of achieving an integrated curriculum expired when Becker left Syracuse, the category of alienation continued to appear and be developed in his writings as a way of summarizing what is undeveloped in human creativity and potential. Besides that he remained friends and a steady letter writing partner with this chaplain, Harvey Bates. This deepened Becker's interest in viewing alienation from the perspective of theology. Becker was especially impressed with the formulations of theologian Paul Tillich (Becker 1964b, 1967, 1968b, 1972, and 1973) and in the coming years Becker also gained an abiding interest in Judaism, the religion of his ethnic origins (Becker 1974a, 1977).

THE SCIENCE OF MAN

What makes people act the way they do was the foundational question for Becker's "Science of Man." In his view, any source, coming from any direction, that aided in answering this question ought to be of interest for the social scientist. His formulations changed in the years of his academic research and writing, but this question remained the focus for his investigations. This essay elucidates several aspects of Becker's proposed science of mankind, concentrating especially on those aspects that are most relevant to psychological and pastoral counselors. To better place Becker's ideas in perspective, a brief outline of his conception of human science might be helpful.

Becker strongly felt that the social sciences had made a terrible mistake in trying to model themselves after the natural sciences. He felt there are distinct differences between the human and natural sciences that made this both inappropriate and self-defeating. In the first place, Becker reacted very strongly against the kind of narrow empiricism that had come to dominate research in the social sciences. In allowing itself to be concerned with smaller and smaller problems just to be able to perform a controlled experiment, the social sciences were forsaking their true calling to be a source of criticism of existing social relations (Becker 1964b, 1971). When that critical edge is removed, the research simply becomes another source for commodity promotion. Becker rejected the notion that eventually all of the small, empirical studies would add up to a true knowledge about human behavior, especially since it was always the human element that this kind of research tried to factor out.

Second, Becker did not think that human behavior was precisely measurable. This was due not to the inadequacy of the tools for measurement but to the nature of the subject itself. Because of this, there could also be no precise predictions in human behavior. This assumes a closed system, and human behavior is an open system (Becker 1971). While Becker was rather lonely in this view during his own time, it has become increasingly accepted as part of the interpretive turn in recent social science research (Rabinow and Sullivan 1987).

Finally, Becker rejected the idea that an abstract and universal science of individual personality could ever be constructed. Since individual personality as an emotionally charged symbol system is formed within a cultural context and incorporates the symbols of that culture, the study of personality development would always have to be culturally specific (Becker 1967).

Becker's vision of a science of human behavior drew specifically on the Enlightenment ideal of a science that would provide some rational basis for determining human goals and providing the means for achieving those goals. In other words, it would be an ideal-real (or utopian) science that did not assume that what humans are empirically determines what humans might become. It would be the study of the relationship between ends and means, a study of why we fall short of our highest ideals and what we can do to remove the barriers to achievement of our highest ideals. This would be the expressed purpose of all areas of the study of human institutions and the effects of these institutions on the individual. Becker saw that human beings impose meaning structures on their experience through the categories of symbols that are given them by their culture. These symbolic meaning systems enable the person to act, but at the same time place constrictions on possible actions (Becker 1968a). An ideal-real social science, therefore, would assist in gaining understanding of these symbolic meaning systems and at the same time point toward a means of transcending these symbolic systems of meaning in the creation of human freedom.

This science would be especially important for a democratic society, for it would seek to place the tools for shaping human possibilities in the hands of individuals themselves. In Becker's view, this kind of science could never be value neutral, as the natural sciences seek to be. The separation of fact and value simply has no place in a science that seeks to empower human beings.

A true science of human behavior would "avoid moving against and negating any point of view . . . if it seems to have in it a core of truthfulness." (Becker 1973, p. xi). There is nothing outside of the field of the study of human behavior if it is grounded in real human experience and interpretation of that experience.

This is not to say that all interpretations must be taken at face value. To the contrary, Becker always distinguished between the experience itself and interpretation of that experience. But he was also aware of the ways in which interpretations tend to devalue and negate real experience in the reductionist mode of "this is nothing but . . ." It was the "nothing but . . ." of this equation that Becker would not accept. The reductionist mode inevitably obscures something, refuses to see something, makes equivalencies where close attention to the differences would be more instructive. This was the basis of Becker's ongoing argument with psychoanalytic theory, which, while pointing toward something undeniably important in understanding human behavior, exemplified the reductionist mode *par excellence.*

Psychoanalysis originally saw itself as an integrative science of human behavior. But psychoanalysis concerned itself centrally with individual behavior. As a social scientist, Becker understood that all individual behavior was rooted in a concrete social and cultural context. His criticism of the psychoanalytic approach, echoing the criticism made by social workers and other applied social science professionals, was that it was too narrow. While classical psychoanalysis pretended to offer a science of human behavior, its first myopia, that is, where it needed extension, stemmed from this exclusive focus on the individual. Individual behavior, as the post-Freudians saw, must be understood as a reaction to a social context. Female hysteria, for example, could not be approached as an individually isolated event. It carried with it the weight of the place of the female in nineteenth-century society—the cultural restrictions upon the creative and intelligent female of that time, the avenues for cultural adaptation, and the reactions of the contemporary creative and intelligent female to those avenues of adaptation. This same approach to mental vulnerabilities must be extended through historical periods in order to gain a fuller understanding of human behavior, both adaptive and maladaptive. In short, Becker insisted that a science of human behavior must be seen first and foremost as a science of man (i.e., the individual) within society (within the cultural *Umwelt* of the times). We come to an understanding of human behavior and human potential only by seeing how specific people adapted themselves to the social and cultural restrictions within which they have had to live.

Once mental illness is understood not primarily as a dysfunction of the individual but rather in terms of the society and culture within which the person lives, a thorough questioning and criticism of the medical model of mental illness is soon to follow. Becker did not dispute that in a minority of cases real, organic dysfunction did occur in mental functioning for which a medically based psychiatry and psychology were necessary. But he strongly questioned the treatment of all mental disorders based on a medical model. He was especially critical of the continuing predominance of the medical model within psychoanalysis.

His thorough questioning of the medical model for treatment of mental illness was the main reason that he received a number of scathing and dismissive reviews for his books in various publications. It was also the reason he was dismissed from teaching psychiatric interns and residents at Syracuse. Having spent more than a century distinguishing and separating themselves from philosophy and the religious care of souls, psychiatry and psychology were not eager to be called back to those roots.

In Becker's writings, there is a recognizable progression in his understanding of the content of this science of mankind, which we will look at in more depth later. In his earliest writings, he used the concept of self-esteem main-

tenance as the unifying core for investigation and understanding (Becker 1962e). How does a person maintain
self-esteem in specific historical and cultural circumstances? What happens when the person is unable to
maintain a sense of self-esteem? What forces of society
foster and inhibit the person's ability to maintain a sense of
self-esteem? Later this core idea was expanded by the
concept of alienation, which was the underside of self-
esteem (Becker 1967). Becker used the concept of alienation to describe degrees of unfulfillment of human
potential and proposed a theory of education based on the
investigation and elucidation of alienation in society.

Throughout this phase of his work, Becker continued
in the optimistic mode of the humanistic Enlightenment in
assuming that at root human striving was neutral or even
good—that human beings would pursue noble goals if
these were available within the social context. This included even the negative aspects of human striving, such
as aggression. Becker felt that because human nature was
essentially malleable, a moral commitment to the perfect-
ibility of human nature was essential to a social science
aimed at the improvement of the individual and society.

In his final works, he came to doubt that human
nature is good. In these writings, which Becker considered
to be his mature work, the concept of self-esteem maintenance was expanded into positive hero striving. Likewise
the underside, alienation, was replaced by the frightened
need to deny one's own mortality (Becker 1973). This shift
is significant. For while alienation is essentially a social
problem that can be overcome, mortality is an ontological
fact of human existence that cannot be overcome. The root
cause of human behavior and human evil is the attempt to
deny, through striving for heroism, what cannot finally be
denied. He was forced to the conclusion that people ag-

gress and kill not only to protect themselves and their loved ones, or because of hatred and rage that form due to the alienating structures of society. People aggress and kill for the pure organismic enjoyment of the act of killing—of standing triumphantly over the corpses of one's victims, defiantly claiming symbolic mastery over death itself. Although Becker retained his hope for improvement of the human condition, he was significantly sobered by this understanding of human evil.

Ernest Becker, therefore, represents a truly post-liberal theorist. Drawn to the study of human behavior by his commitment to improving individual and social life, he was finally forced to conclude that the inevitability of progress in human history was open to great doubt, and that, furthermore, there is a worm at the core of human nature, a frantic struggle within the breast of the human being, requiring not simply a social scientific response but a spiritual and theological response as well.

2

Human Ego Development— Primary Concepts

*We miss
parts of our character when they're cut,
but those lost aspects still hang there,
like ghosts.*

S. J. Marks

THE BIOLOGICAL BACKGROUND

What makes people act the way they do? Ernest Becker
approached this question as a trained anthropologist. He
utilized the tools of social science, of psychology and
sociology, informed by cross-cultural studies, and he was
grounded in evolutionary biology.

Human beings are animals and share with all animal
species in the movement of species evolution. Much scientific and popular literature seems to assume that human
behavior can best be explained by studying animal behavior. Terms such as *nesting instinct, herd behavior, terri-
toriality, and natural aggression* have become established
as part of our everyday vocabulary.

Becker recognized that human behavior carried with
it the face of its evolutionary background. However, he

rejected the determinism of biology as destiny, which often underlies this point of view (Becker 1962a,e). All animals are creatures of action, and for nonhuman animals, their actions are firmly set by nature. Human beings, by contrast, are almost devoid of guiding instincts. We must learn how to act in our environment. In Becker's presentation of human ego development, biological facts determine the parameters, to be sure. But biology is quickly superseded by the sociocultural environment in shaping the human being. Yet biology does have a very important influence on culture as well.

Especially important for understanding early human ego development is the long gestation period that human beings share with all of the higher primates (Becker 1962e). In human beings this is most pronounced. After nine long months in the womb, a human baby is born. Yet this baby is totally helpless, incapable of satisfying even its most basic survival needs. Other mammals birth young who are also helpless. But within a few minutes, hours, days, or at most weeks, these young are mobile in seeking food sources and beginning to fend for themselves. Human offspring, in contrast, spend months and even years in a more or less completely passive state in terms of survival needs. They are totally dependent on having these needs met for them by others.

Anyone who has had to deal with a screaming baby may want to dispute just how passive the child is in getting its needs met! Yet the fact remains that, while able to signal its need for care, the human infant is unable to meet those needs alone for many months and years. From an interspecies perspective, we could say that in relation to its ability to survive, the human infant is born many years prematurely. In Becker's view, this long period of dependence is of central importance for beginning to comprehend what makes human behavior different from that of other animal species (Becker 1962e).

In other animal species, a very direct and immediate relationship exists between environmental stimulus and the organic response to that stimulus. We refer to this immediate stimulus-response sequence as instinctual behavior. The organism seems to be programmed by nature to respond in set ways to stimulation in its environment. The more predictable and monolithic the response to a given stimulation, the more we call upon the word *instinct* to account for it. The less predictable and varied the response, the more likely we are to assign a degree of choice to the behavior. It makes little or no sense to use words like *will* or *choice* to describe, for example, the response of a one-celled animal to the stimulus of food in its environment. But it does make sense to use such words to describe the response of the family dog to the stimulus of a thrown stick. Sometimes the dog fetches and sometimes not.

The ability to delay response to environmental stimulation, to consider possible actions, and to choose among possible actions before acting increases as we move up the evolutionary ladder (Becker 1962e). In the higher primates, it is even possible to delay response and to choose behavior that violates what might be considered actions helpful to the survival of the organism. Cat owners who have tried to switch to cheaper brands of cat food can testify to the extreme degree to which the feline is capable of delaying the satisfaction of its own hunger so as to engage in a battle of wills in expressing its dissatisfaction with the change in food.

In human beings, this ability to delay response and to choose among possible courses of actions reaches its highest point in the evolution of species. The human being, in fact, may even choose a course of action that allows the continued existence of the symbolic self at the expense of the organic self—for example, in a hunger strike. This kind of possibility is unique to the human species. Understanding how such a being develops out of a crying and grasping infant, interested only in the satisfaction of its bodily needs, is therefore a central interest in the pursuit of comprehending human behavior.

THE ROLE OF ANXIETY

In all of the higher primates, close care is required for the young. Evolution has created a bond between parent and young in these species that is not found in other animals. Without this bond, which is the parental response to the helplessness of the young, the species would not survive. There is evidence that this bond is learned in each generation. Little ones deprived of warm care find it difficult or impossible as adults to establish that bond with their own offspring (Schwartz 1986).

The need for close, warm body care, for affection and praise, is an established and essential requirement for human infants. Without it the infant cannot thrive. The infant continues in this need to one extent or another throughout childhood. This need for continued care is one fundamental component of the child's motivation. The other component is closely related. It is anxiety, aroused by the child's fear of abandonment by its primary caregivers.

A human infant has no developed sense of self. It is totally dependent on caregivers for survival, and experiences life on the level of a cycle of physical needs and physical satisfactions. When an infant receives adequate care, there is little delay between the time that the infant signals its physical discomfort and having the care given and the discomfort relieved. The caregivers are experienced as an extension of the infant itself.

As the child grows older, the time between the signal of discomfort and the receiving of comforting care grows longer. Due to the delay between the stimulus and the response, the child begins to recognize that the caregivers are not simply an extension of the child. The caregivers have an existence that is separate from the child, and the child begins to experience its first form of anxiety—the anxiety of being abandoned by the caregivers. The child realizes that techniques must be learned to coax the caregivers into action. These techniques also reassure the child that it has not been abandoned and thus relieves these earliest pangs of anxiety. One of the earliest techniques a child learns is to scream and cry. A child may use this technique to cause the appearance of the caregivers even though suffering from no immediate physical need. In this way, the child gains the assurance and sense of security that it has not been abandoned by the caregivers.

All of the techniques the child uses to gain assurance of the continuation of care are physical. These range from facial expressions to noise making. The growing child uses its body as a medium for assurance of continued care.

As growth progresses the child starts to learn that not everything it does with its body is equally effective in coaxing the caregivers into the desired response. The growing child learns that some uses of its body as a medium are not appreciated by the caregivers and do not result in loving, cooing, and smiling faces being thrust into the child's view. This is probably very confusing to the child, since to the child all physical exertions, all uses of its physical being as a medium, are equal. Yet some actions provoke an opposite response in the caregivers than what the child expected and hoped to receive. Their voices become loud and harsh. Their faces show obvious signs of displeasure, again provoking in the child that early anxiety of abandonment by the caregivers.

In time the child learns that the urge to act out on certain impulses needs to be curbed in favor of a higher goal of pleasing the caregivers and continuing to bask in the assurance of their continued care. In the course of this learning process, the child begins to form its most primitive sense of self, of ego, as an organism that is not tied simply to an automatic cycle of stimulus and response, but as an organism that can imagine itself acting in various ways and then choosing among them. At this most rudimentary stage of development, we already see the growing child making its self an object of thought to itself, which is the first stage of early ego development (Becker 1962e).

It is important to notice here that ego development occurs as a result of negotiating frustrations of desires and the experiences of opposition in the child's environment. Our very perception of an object, registering it in our field of experience, is based on the ability to respond to the object. If gratification were always immediate, we would hardly register the experience in our consciousness, for there is no delay in response that causes the experience to be noted in our consciousness (Becker 1964b). If the child were to experience no frustration or opposition at all in its environment, it would have no means of experiencing its self as something distinct from that which is outside the self. On the other hand, for healthy ego development the frustrations and opposition cannot be totally overwhelming either, for then there is no chance to negotiate toward satisfaction. It is the negotiating process, even at the prelinguistic stage, that is the path for healthy ego development. The ego expands by confronting opposition, delaying response, testing its powers in the face of that opposition, and then acting on those powers to deal with the opposition.

The long gestation period and the total helplessness of the human newborn create the conditions under which the initial anxieties of the infant are directly related to loss of the caregivers. The growing child learns to negotiate the responses of the caregivers. Using its physical body as the medium, the child's overwhelming desire is to please its caregivers and therefore to assure itself that it has not been and will not be abandoned by the caregivers. It is this negotiating process, learning that some physical exertions cause a desirable response on the part of the caregivers while others do not, that is the mechanism for the rudimentary development of the child's ego, its sense of itself as separate from its caregivers and its environment.

The need for continued care, for a close relationship with its primary caregivers, is the very source of the anxiety of object loss, of abandonment, in the child (Becker 1962e). This initial anxiety is strengthened as the child begins to experience the fact that its caregivers are not automatons commanded by the child's will. Delays in gratification, and above all being told "no!" provoke in the child the anxiety of abandonment. The child needs to avoid anxiety-provoking situations for its own continued sense of well-being. The child learns through experience that by refusing certain urges, refusing to act on some impulses, anxiety-provoking situations can be avoided. The child begins to learn that holding itself in check, curbing organismic urges to explore and expand in all directions, is necessary to avoid provoking its greatest anxiety, the anxiety of abandonment.

The child is already engaged in a process that according to Becker is one of the great ironies of human existence. That is, that in order to avoid overwhelming anxiety, anxiety that is crippling to ego expansion and development, the self assumes the task of being its own limiter. Repression is carried out largely by the ego itself in response to its environment and becomes the very mechanism by which the ego learns to avoid anxiety and to allow itself continued growth and expansion in at least some areas.

Significantly, however, the areas in which the ego does allow itself expansion are not those areas of the ego's own choosing. They are prescribed by the desires and values of the primary caregivers and, later, by the sociocultural environment. The irony in this, rooted in the very nature of being human, of being an animal that strives for its own sense of well-being by avoiding anxiety, is that the ego is bound to a process of conforming itself to the image of the other as the very condition for its own continued growth and expansion (Becker 1962e). This process is embedded even in the prelinguistic phase of child development, long before the child has any notion of what is happening to it. As will be seen, this carries lifelong consequences.

In the next stage of development, the child begins to master a completely new kind of medium for negotiation. It is that of a symbol system, the use of language. During this stage the rudimentary sense of self that resulted from the use of the body as the negotiating medium is exponentially increased. The self becomes embedded in this symbol system and takes on a form that is truly and uniquely human (Becker 1962e).

The earliest experience the child has of a self is one that is a reflection of the attitudes toward the child of the caregivers. The child's perceptions, the child's consciousness, is initially united with that of its caregivers and is therefore fundamentally a product of the social environment. In the early stages of using language, the child will even refer to itself primarily in the third person. It may be some time before the child learns to use first-person pronouns, and even then the accusative "me!" and the genitive "mine!" will be used long before the nominative "I."

By the time the child learns the proper use of "I," a significant step in ego development has been achieved. The child has developed the ability to abstract and to see itself as an abstraction, as a first-person linguistic construction. As far as we can tell, humans are the only species that are able as a matter of course to develop this sense of abstract ego awareness. The human ego, in other words, takes shape linguistically, and it is the use of language that sets humans apart from other animal species (Becker 1962e).

MAINTENANCE OF SELF-ESTEEM

The developing human ego seeks to avoid and master anxiety. Anxiety is rooted in the very precariousness of human existence. It is not possible for a human being with normal mental capacities to live without anxiety, for anxiety is a basic response to the actual conditions of human existence. What the ego is able to do is to develop specific defense mechanisms against the onslaught of overwhelming anxiety. The defense mechanisms allow the ego to deal with anxiety in manageable doses, thus allowing the ego to maintain its sense of mastery, its sense of forward movement.

Drawing on the psychoanalytic literature, Becker (1962e) wrote of three main mechanisms of defense that develop very early and continue throughout life:

Denial—the ability of the ego to simply ignore painful and
    anxiety-provoking situations;
Projection—the ability of the ego to ascribe anxious
    thoughts and feelings to others rather than to the self;
Repression—the ability of the ego to block out and erase
    anxiety-provoking experiences from the realm of con-
    sciousness.

In using each of these ego defenses, the self protects
itself from massive and overwhelming anxiety by binding
the anxiety and then allowing the ego to call it up in small-
enough doses that the ego can master it. Much of what
transpires in the play world of children and the thought
world of adolescents and adults is exactly this process of
calling up and facing manageable doses of anxiety. The
mastery of anxiety is essentially what Becker means by
self-esteem. It is through the mastery of anxiety that the ego
is able to maintain its sense of forward movement. When
the ego is unable to master anxiety, it will feel overwhelmed, blocked, bogged down. Furthermore, by employing these mechanisms of defense, the ego creates a reservoir
of material of which the conscious self is unaware. This
material forms the content of the unconscious, the id.
Becker saw it as one of the major achievements of psychoanalysis to have developed processes whereby the content
of the unconscious could be identified and explored.

Although in his later work Becker felt that the concept
was too vague, he posited self-esteem maintenance as an
overall paradigmatic framework for understanding human
behavior. We will later explore his refinements of the idea.
But for now let us look at what this concept has to tell us
about early human ego development.

Self-esteem maintenance is a dynamic concept. One
does not achieve self-esteem and then stop. Life moves on

and the developing ego constantly confronts new objects and experiences. A healthy developing self is naturally drawn to novelty because the ego grows by new experiences—it feeds on new experiences, so to speak. We admire the natural curiosity of children and a child who exhibits no sense of curiosity, who draws back from all novelty, would be a cause for great concern. Nevertheless, all novelty contains within it the possibility of provoking anxiety. A sense of self-esteem is maintained as the self learns to confront new objects and new experiences and to draw on its powers to master the anxiety that the novelty provokes. This allows incorporation of that object or experience into the repertoire of the ego, to be called upon at will in later confrontations with new objects or experiences. Becker wrote of a three-stage process for maintaining the sense of forward movement necessary for healthy ego development.

The first stage is manipulation (Becker 1964b). When confronted with a new object or experience, the initial response is the organismic urge to act upon it. In toddlers this is expressed very bodily—touch it, pick it up, chew on it. The repertoire of the toddler's ego is still quite limited. An older child will have a wider reservoir of possible responses, perhaps already exhibiting the restrictions that the ego places on the organism—it's red and glows . . . caution! It may be hot! An adult may act upon the new object or experience in purely mental/symbolic form. When confronted with novelty, the initial human urge is to act upon it, to manipulate it in some form.

The second stage is that of seeking meaning in the novel. The problem of meaning in the face of the objective precariousness of human existence contains a deeply existential aspect to it which will be explored later. At this point, *meaning* denotes the individual's ability to call up responses to objects and experiences that allow the self to continue its sense of forward movement. Novelty provokes anxiety and the self reaches into its repertoire of responses, calling forth those responses that allow the ego to avoid anxiety and attain some sense of mastery over the novel situation. A confronting object or experience about which one can draw no appropriate response whatsoever cannot have meaning. It is literally meaningless. This may extend even to the level of finding existence itself—that is, continuing organismic being as the confronting object—to be totally meaningless.

Again, a toddler's repertoire is limited—touch it, pick it up, suck on it. Hence the confusion when it burns, is too heavy to move, tastes terrible. An older child is already learning to abstract and also to seek social approval for its responses. A rolled-up rug, for example, long and just low enough to straddle with one leg, might call up the response of "horsey" in such a child. The abstract qualities of "horsey" may be the only meaning the object has in the child's world. Finding that throwing or kicking the red, round object earns more praise from caregivers than sucking on it, the child learns new ways to respond meaningfully to the abstraction of "ball" (an abstraction that, perhaps, will then be painfully refined when the child first confronts a holiday tree ornament).

By adulthood the abstraction process is well developed and meaning itself may by then have become an abstract notion. At this second stage, however, meaning simply connotes the ability of the ego to draw up from its repertoire of responses those guidelines for manipulation that allow the self to act upon the experience of novelty in ways that anxiety is avoided and mastery is achieved.

The third step is self-esteem. This step in the process is not strictly behavioral but symbolic and psychological.

As the self reflects on its achievements during stages one and two, it is confirmed in the view that it is an able executive living in an environment in which it has appropriate powers. The ego feels good about itself, sees itself as a locus of value, and adds this experience of mastery to the expanding repertoire from which it will draw in future confrontations with novelty.

In real life this process is precarious at every point. There are innumerable ways in which this continually moving process of manipulation, meaning, self-esteem and further manipulation can break down. A new experience may call up associations so full of anxiety that the ego is literally swamped and cannot lay hold of it. It may evoke an abstraction that is so far removed from the object that it is impossible to act upon the object on the basis of that abstraction. Furthermore, even when an object transaction has been successful, the resulting sense of self-esteem remains vulnerable to deflation by the reactions of others—think of the beaming American traveler who announces to his more knowledgeable friends that the suite in his Paris hotel is even equipped with a footwasher in the bathroom.

Caregivers impart the initial funding of self-value through warm praise and continued affection. But the fact is that even in the most secure of circumstances, self-esteem skates on very thin ice above embarrassment, shame, guilt, deflation, a sense of being blocked and bogged down—all manifestations of basic anxiety. Real, lived human experience is a shifting patchwork of triumph in some areas and defeat in others. Self-esteem maintenance, avoiding and mastering anxiety sufficiently to have a continued sense of forward movement, is a vital juggling act in which the cost of failure can be literally one's life. In Becker's view a human life without mechanisms of defense, the mechanisms that allow one to navigate in the sea of overwhelming anxiety, is quite simply unimaginable (Becker 1973).

THE OEDIPAL TRANSITION

Becker rejected the instinct theory of Freud and insisted that human beings can best be viewed for practical purposes as devoid of both sexual and aggressive instincts. Furthermore, while Freud (1930) saw these most basic instinctual drives as fundamentally antisocial in nature, Becker believed that the human ego or sense of self is primarily a social product.

Becker recognized fully the contribution of Freud to understanding human behavior. Any new theory that would be considered at all adequate could not ignore Freud. It would have to incorporate Freud's ideas into a broader synthesis (Becker 1969). Freud saw the discovery of the Oedipus complex as his greatest achievement. Becker preferred to speak of an oedipal transition that did not rely on instinctual drives as the motivating force for personality development.

In Becker's view, what psychoanalysis discovered was the symbolic nature of human self-esteem, whose contours are shaped in the individual during the oedipal transition period in which the person learns to trade physiological nurturing for the psychological nurturing of the symbol system. This is why Becker speaks of an oedipal transition rather than an Oedipus complex, favoring a model in which the oedipal transition is a time in which the child must learn to seek and be satisfied with continued parental involvement on a psychological/ symbolic level, rather than on a direct physiological level. It is a culturally specific process and is the beginning of the process of socialization. During the oedipal transition the child is being changed from a primarily biological actor to a primarily social actor (Becker 1962e).

Psychoanalytic theory outlines stages of development focused on body orifices as erotic centers. Working from a fully transactional and existential frame of reference, Becker utilized the same stages. However, in Becker's view these stages do not revolve around instinctual drives. They are viewed as centers for the child's relationship to its adult caregivers (Becker 1973). They are not phases in libidinal organization, in other words, but stages in socialization.

The oral stage takes place during the time before the ego of the infant is totally differentiated from the mother. The mouth is the center of its relationship with the mother. During the anal stage, the child becomes aware of its body as an object. It becomes aware that in order to gain a sense of mastery, the body itself must be mastered. To avoid the anxiety of abandonment and maintain an ongoing warm and supportive relationship with its caregivers, the child learns that especially the bowels must be mastered and controlled. The child's relationship with adults during this phase naturally comes to center on the anus and its products. Anal play is a tool of the ego in mastering in manageable doses the anxiety of learning body control and the child will be quite proud in showing off its accomplishment of defecating in the right place. It is a demonstration of ego control over its own body casing. The child is learning to earn love and support from its caregivers, accepting the frustrations of denying itself immediate physical gratification in order to maintain a positive overall relationship with the parents on an increasingly symbolic level.

During the final phase, the phallic stage, the child is forcefully faced with the full implications of exchanging biological (body) meanings for social (symbolic) meanings. Throughout the oedipal transition, spurred by anxiety avoidance, the child is in the process of giving up bodily gratifications in favor of the security of maintaining adult care and attention. In this final stage, ambivalence is most acute. Propelled by the increasing functional mastery of the developing ego, the child is at the same time restrained by the needs of the self for continued care and affection (Becker 1962e).

The oedipal transition is not a straightforward and unidirectional process. It is a process of learning by which the child is inducted into symbolic performance in relation to its caregivers. It is a training period in which the child changes its primary mode of self-esteem maintenance in relation to its caregivers. Initially basking in erotic body closeness, the child emerges from this process able to maintain self-esteem on the basis of living within the symbolic world of the parents. Yet to the child, much of this symbolic world remains a mystery. Therefore, the child is in a process of being weaned from physical satisfactions that it does understand and being taught symbolic satisfactions that it does not understand. This is yet another basis for the ambivalence and rebellion that the child feels toward the whole process.

The parental values and modes of perception that the child accepts as its own during this period are largely habitual. They are not freely chosen by the ego and the ego remains unaware of alternatives. They become automatic patterns of the ego to avoid the anxiety aroused by displeasing the parents. The very process, therefore, by which the child becomes a symbolic performer, becomes human, further limits the conscious choices of the ego in relation to the broad spectrum of possible behaviors. The child's restrictions of behavior to please its parents progressively come to include symbolic behavior and symbolic pleasing. This necessarily ties the child to the same limitations that form the world of its parents. A person's character comes to reflect the peculiar perceptions, behaviors, values, and anxieties of his or her caregivers. The study of character types is predicated on the fact that, in light of the limited range of behavioral styles available to avoid and master the anxieties of the human condition, there emerge certain broad and identifiable character modes among human beings, which tend to be passed down through families from generation to generation (Becker 1973).

SOCIALIZATION—ADAPTING TO CULTURE

Becker drew on a broad spectrum of social science literature to construct his view of culture and society and how socialization is an extension of the early training of the child. We will return to this subject later. For now a preliminary sketch will help us understand the operations of early socialization as it relates to the individual.

By the time the child has successfully come through the oedipal transition, the child has learned to maintain self-esteem in a symbolic mode, by accepting the peculiar behavioral style of the caregivers, the parents and family members. Although the process is not straightforward and the acceptance on the part of the child is ambivalent, it is a most important initial step in socialization. In socialization, primary anxiety is utilized to tutor the child in the cultural symbol world. The primary anxiety of abandonment is steadily transformed into the mature adult abhorrence of wrong behavior (Becker 1962e). The child accepts this disciplining in the interest of becoming an independent cultural actor. The unconscious, formed by the mechanisms of defense in early training, expands to include the taboos of the culture and society in which the individual is raised.

From a psychological perspective, what has happened to the child through this process of becoming a "symbolic self" is that a superego or conscience has been formed. Superego simply refers to the idea that from that point on, the child will gain a sense of self-value from doing the right and proper thing as an habitual course of action, even though the person will have no immediate awareness from where the inner voice urging such behavior comes. From this learning process, the child enters into the wider social environment where rules, customs, and a means-ends schema of action are embedded into the automatic behavioral patterns of the person. In the cultural world this new mode of maintaining self-esteem will be further inculcated and reinforced. Once the superego of the individual is firmly implanted, the person's mind is claimed for society. "It's just the way it's done" becomes the tune to which most people will dance for the duration of life.

In Becker's view, further socialization in the cultural milieu means above all a direct continuation of the self narrowing its freedom and possibilities in exchange for being able to view itself as a locus of value in a world of meaning. The process by which the child has limited its ego strivings so as to find its place in the family order and thus assure itself of the continued care and affection of its caregivers is extended into the social and cultural environment. By learning to transact in culturally prescribed and socially accepted modes, the self finds its place in this environment and thus assures itself of its continued symbolic value. This identity is built on symbolic social performance and it is the ability to perform in the proper social role that solidifies one's sense of self-esteem. A social identity can only be earned from other people, those who are in positions of superior power and who introduce the individual into the new social symbolic world (1964b).

Culture forms the environmental shell within which a person's personality will develop. In this environment, the individual seeks to maintain the process of assuring the self of its primary value. The function of culture and society is to give its people a theater and script to maintain this process. Culture and society, therefore, can be seen as an amalgam of pathways for creating and sustaining individual symbolic meaning.

Maintenance of symbolic meaning assumes the ability to repress anxiety. In the social world, disorder is a major anxiety-provoking factor. Growing up in society is fundamentally a process of learning how to act in an unpredictable environment. This is a peculiar problem for an anxiety-prone animal such as the human being. A certain amount of control and stability is achieved when one learns to correctly play his or her social role (Becker 1964a). The viability of a culture for the individual is predicated on the stability of social transactions. Culture has to provide safety as well as avenues for self-esteem.

Status and role are fundamental concepts in the working of society and culture (Becker 1962e). For the individual to maintain a sense of value and forward movement, the primary anxiety of abandonment, loneliness, and symbolic deflation must be repressed. The rules and order of society are requisite to the ability to repress anxiety. Simple self-preservation dictates that the person have some means of predicting the behavior of other people. Status and role serve to make social encounters predictable and dependable. Status and role tell the individual how to act in specific social situations and also what behaviors can be expected from others. By providing the rules and guidelines for interaction, social and cultural conventions are essentially scripts for self-esteem maintenance.

Socialization continues the learning process that was begun in early childhood training in both its positive and negative aspects. On the positive side the dependence of the child on its primary caregivers for security and feelings of self-worth are transferred to the wider symbol system of the culture and society. The ability to sustain a symbolic sense of self-value and forward movement that is not dependent on the direct and binding ties of the relationship with primary caregivers allows for a new measure of freedom for the individual. The stage of social interaction makes ego expansion possible on a scale larger than could ever be achieved only within the immediate family circle. Actions shared and reinforced by larger groups of people are much more convincing to the individual and therefore provide an even more solid sense of purpose and meaning. Because the parameters of child-training configurations are set by cultural norms, oedipal training contours the child's personality for membership in his or her particular culture and society, shaping the child to feel comfortable and at home in the institutions of that very society.

On the negative side, however, it must be noted that the mechanism of culture and society for achieving this transference to the broader symbol system remains the manipulation of the individual's primary anxiety. The commitment of the person to the social and cultural meanings of his or her environment continues to be based on the foundation of anxiety. Even for the most grounded of persons living in the most integrated of societies, this river of anxiety runs under the surface, and the denial, projection, and repression utilized to avoid this anxiety increase in the same measure as that of possible ego expansion.

While in one sense we can speak of the entrance onto the social stage of action as an opening up and widening of the possibilities for individual ego expansion, this is actually achieved only by a further narrowing down, distortion, and skewing of the person's perceptions about the true nature of human reality. Becker went so far as to call this a process of "reinstinctivization," a process in which the human animal, though born devoid of instinctual rules for behavior, becomes totally embedded in automatic behavioral styles over which he or she has no more control than do lemmings running to the sea (Becker 1968a). Furthermore, the person becomes bound by an extra measure of anxiety to the peculiar worldview, meanings and values of his or her particular culture and society. One reason that cross-cultural studies can be so threatening is exactly because seeing that other people are so different (and yet happy and content) awakens in people the sense that the norms, values, and meanings of their particular culture and society are largely fictitious and arbitrary, opening one up in turn to the river of anxiety that flows beneath the surface of our serenity.

Technologically, through travel and communications, we have advanced to the point where daily confrontation with the fictitious and arbitrary nature of our cultural norms, meanings, and values is simply unavoidable for most people. Yet it is not at all clear that we have advanced psychologically to the point we are able to control the urges toward violent xenophobic lashing out that bubbles up from the deepest levels of our psyche when forced to confront the anxiety at the root of our social existence. This has left us with what might be called the dilemma of postmodern social consciousness: acceptance of uncertainty and anxiety on the one hand, or the security of willful myopic intolerance on the other hand. This is the dilemma to which Ernest Becker returned again and again in his writings, both in terms of its implications for humanity as a species and for the prospects of mental health in modern society.

THE SOCIAL/CLINICAL PICTURE

In Ernest Becker's formulation of mental hygiene, the normal is neurotic. Although he stated this somewhat provocatively and ironically, he meant it to be taken seriously. Mental health is seen as an ideal-typical construct that might be relatively approximated but never actually achieved. (See Figure 2–1.) Repression comes from within. It is self-repression. All human beings repress to one extent or another and life without repression would be intolerable. Of the normal person Becker wrote, "If we say that the average man narrows down 'just about right,' we have to ask who this average man is. . . . all through history it is the 'normal, average men' who, like locusts, have laid waste to the world in order to forget themselves" (Becker 1973, p. 187).

If "normal mental health" is a social construction, how does it happen that some people are thought to require special care from mental health professionals? How does it happen that some people lose their freedom, are incarcerated in prisons or psychiatric hospitals, because of their mental condition?

Very early in his career, Becker published an instructive article that outlined some anthropological and philosophical reflections on the problem of mental health (Becker 1961b). In this article Becker drew on the anthropological literature to demonstrate that mental health, normality, far from being an absolute concept, consists

THE SOCIAL / CLINICAL PICTURE

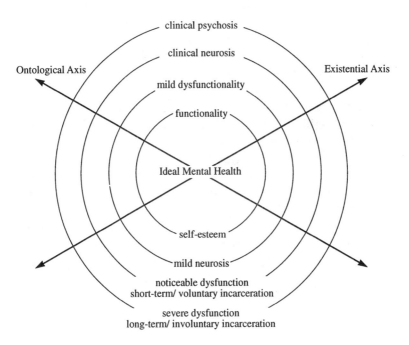

Figure 2–1

mainly of the appropriate use of public logic, that is, the logic shared by most people in the society, in everyday actions and perceptions. Mental illness, on the other hand, consists mainly of the inability to utilize public logic in everyday perceptions and behavior.

According to Becker, public logic is necessary for survival. The inability to use public knowledge in everyday perceptions and behavior will finally end in self-destruction of the person. So-called primitive societies were very tolerant of the mentally ill, those who employed mainly private logic in everyday perceptions and behaviors, and allowed them to live as much as possible as part of the society as a whole, because they were also very tolerant of the self-destruction that this style of living entailed. The sanctity of public knowledge, its utter convincing quality, was assured by simply observing the end to which those who significantly deviated from it came.

Modern societies are not tolerant of the self-destruction (suicide, starvation, burning or cutting oneself, and so forth) that is entailed by the use of private logic in everyday perceptions and behaviors. On the other hand, such societies protect the sanctity of their public logic by maintaining an equal intolerance of those who employ a private logic in perception and behavior. They are treated, and if need be, incarcerated. Treatment and/or incarceration is not, therefore, a statement about one's mental health in any absolute sense. It is rather a statement of how far one has strayed from the public logic within modern society.

3

Expansion, Anxiety, and Evil

Where there's silence and absolute calm,
what have we to do
with passionate words?
They make no sense at all.

S. J. Marks

THE OEDIPAL PROJECT

What makes people act the way they do? Becker considered Freud's major contribution to be the identification of the Oedipus complex as the mechanism by which the superego, the internalization of the demands and prohibitions of the caregivers, and subsequently society are implanted during the course of individual psychological development (Becker 1969). Freud related this development to instinctive sexual drive, which does not refer strictly to genital functions but rather to the entire range of pleasure-seeking urges, beginning in infancy. The sexual drive is expressed in a wide variety of activities with a wide variety of objects. In Freudian theory, however, it remains the key concept in personality development and organization.

Although any part of the body may be a source of pleasure, the mouth, anus, and genitals are seen as the particular locations for erotic pleasure. These erogenous zones are each connected to a particular bodily function that is necessary for survival—eating, defecating, reproducing. Erotic pleasure stemming from these zones is therefore seen as integral to the instinctual drive of self-preservation. The child progresses from mainly oral satisfaction to anal satisfaction and finally to genital satisfaction. At that stage of development, Freud postulated an overtly sexual attraction to the mother (Laplanche and Pontalis 1973).

The child originally identifies with both parents. However, at the point that the (male) child becomes overtly sexually attracted to the mother, the child begins to see the father as a rival for the mother's attention. The result is a strong antagonism toward the father, a desire to eliminate the father from the scene. This desire to be rid of the father and to take full possession of the mother is what Freud referred to as the Oedipus complex.

The father is physically overpowering to the child and the child feels itself endangered by a continuing state of antagonism toward the father. So long as the child continues to desire sexual possession of the mother, the antagonism will continue. The child must therefore repress the sexual desire out of fear of the father's revenge. The child must renounce the mother as an object of sexual desire and in this way again identify with both parents. This renunciation of sexual desire for the other is a capitulation to and internalization of the prohibitions of the adult world. The reidentification of the child with both parents is achieved only by the child's willingness to accept parental and adult prohibitions. It is during this stage of reidentification with both parents that the child develops a superego, the internal voice of parental and adult prohibition.

Ernest Becker was both attracted to and repelled by this explanation of the origins of conscience in the individual. On the one hand, he was quite sure that the development of conscience was intimately connected to relations between the child and its caregivers. He felt that Freud had pointed toward a central issue involved in understanding human development and human behavior (Becker 1972). On the other hand, he was also quite sure that Freud was wrong in terms of his theory of instinctual drives. Becker suggested that this was a reflection of nineteenth-century biologism and not of a well-rounded theory of human behavior (Becker 1973).

Becker rejected the idea of the frustration of inner drives and instincts as the motivating force in human behavior. For Freud, the human being is fundamentally antisocial. The most base of inner urges are seen as prior to and usually more powerful than the refining influence of society. Society and the individual are on the most fundamental level perpetually at odds. He reduced interpersonal behavior to the base animal level of satisfactions. Again, Becker saw in this reductionism the prejudices of nineteenth-century science and philosophy rather than a broadly empirical view of human existence.

Becker did not think that one had to resort to a theory of innate aggressive and sexual drives and their frustrations to account for the implantation of the superego. Nothing more needed to be assumed about the basic motivations of the child than the need for closeness, affection, and continued care (Becker 1968b). These motivations are essentially social in character and not antisocial. Becker wrote not of an Oedipus complex but of an oedipal transition, a transition by which the child comes to ex-

change body-based involvement on the part of the caregivers for continued parental involvement on a psychological and symbolic level. But beyond that, Becker
also wrote of an oedipal project that continues as a life
project (Becker 1973).

In the course of the oedipal transition, the child comes
to see the body as an object to be controlled in the interest
of symbolic modes of self-esteem maintenance (Becker
1972). This process is begun in the anal stage and continues into the phallic stage. The child, in effect, coaxes the
caregivers into continuing closeness, affection, and care by
demonstrating through actions that it understands the
need to take control of body demands and is increasingly
able to do so. The child also demonstrates to itself its own
worthiness of continued parental care by testing its ability
to deny the body, delaying gratification of body cravings
until the proper time as prescribed by the adult world of
symbolic and psychological meanings. Eventually the
child may even play games of body mastery when there is
no adult around to give praise for the act. Certainly the
child's notion is that adults know everything that happens,
whether they are present or absent. This type of play also
displays the child's need to master the anxiety of abandonment by continually assuring itself that it is indeed able to
control the body on a continuing basis.

The body becomes an object for the child's self-
control. The child is pushed by anxiety avoidance into the
symbolic world of adult meanings. Entrance into this
world depends on the child's ability to gain increasing
control over the demands of the body—to delay bodily
satisfactions and channel the gratification of those bodily
cravings into forms, times, and places that accord with the
symbol world of adult meanings. The child feels that if it is
not able to do this, it faces the displeasure of the parents, a

displeasure whose ultimate form is abandonment and annihilation.

During this transitional period, the body as object represents the vehicle for demonstrating successful entry into the adult world of symbolic meanings. But it also represents the major and primary threat to the child's sense of ego mastery. The demands of the body can simply overwhelm a young child to the extent that the child is unable to maintain constant mastery and control (Becker 1962e, 1964b). Furthermore, the child in this transitional state is torn between the earlier method of maintaining self-esteem based on immediate gratification of bodily demands and the new, symbolic method of maintaining self-esteem (avoiding object-loss anxiety) through demonstrated ego mastery of the body. The trade-off sometimes simply does not seem worth the struggle. The body is experienced both as a source of joy and pleasure and as a threatening source of deep shame and anxiety. The self-scolding of a child for temporarily losing control of the body—for soiling its pants, for forbidden touching, for eating before the appropriate time—will often be much more severe and deprecatory than the admonitions of the caregivers. The child is horrified by its own animal condition and in scolding this animal part of its nature severely the child regains the sense that the symbolic self, the "true me," will have mastery over the animal.

In Becker's view, the fact that urine and feces, menstrual blood, bodily orifices and appendages, sexual gestures, and the like seem to be at the root of human guilt and anxiety is not because of instinctual aggressive or sexual drives. Still less does it have to do with primal patricide, incestual urges, and fear of castration (Becker 1973). Becker suggested on the contrary that these things seem to be at the root of human guilt and anxiety because,

to the child in that transitional state, these things represent the immediate and concrete awareness the child has
of the body/animal side of being human. They are the
concrete and physical elements that point toward the hard
fact of animality—animality that at that stage of development is the child's primary threat to demonstrated ego
mastery and continued self-esteem.

Thus the Freudian theory of the Oedipus complex is
too drastically and narrowly defined in terms of sexual
drives and competitiveness. One must appreciate Freud's
insistence on maintaining a body-based psychology in the
face of some alternative postulations of an ethereal soul
that is only temporarily housed in the body. Psychoanalysis had to keep a firm this-worldly grip on its subject
matter. However the dogged sexual reductionism of classic
psychoanalysis undermined its scientific value from the
other side. In short, the sexual theory explains both too
much and too little about human motivation. Becker
hoped that by recasting the oedipal theory in terms of more
current understandings of human behavior coming from
other disciplines that he could achieve an equally this-
worldly theory that was not prone to the strict sexual
reductionism of classical psychoanalysis.

In Becker's transactional and existential reconstruction of the oedipal transition, the body/ego dualism that
emerges tends to define the problem of living itself. The
child encounters this first as it moves to gain entrance into
the adult world of symbolic meaning. But it is a life
project—the oedipal transition leads into the lifelong oedipal project. This dualism is characterized by ego expansion on the one hand and safe anxiety avoidance on the
other. The developing ego seeks to expand, become recognized, and mark its significance in the world of symbolic
meaning. At the same time, extending too far into the new

and unknown inevitably arouses the anxiety of loneliness, of object-loss and abandonment, of annihilation. To allay this anxiety, the person seeks the comfort of shared meanings, of parental and group affirmation, of solid grounding in the performance of socially prescribed demonstrations of ego mastery over the animal nature. This solid grounding, however, carries with it its own anxieties. For the developing ego has the need to separate and develop independence. To simply accept passively the prescriptions of others leads to the anxiety of annihilation by being swallowed up, remaining undifferentiated as an individual creator of meaning (Becker 1972).

The oedipal transition period is the child's first confrontation with the paradox and ambivalence of human existence in the world of symbolic meaning. Will the child be controlled and directed by others? Or will the child become its own center of meaning and symbolic creation? Will the child be an active or passive player in the world of symbolic meaning?

We have already seen that in Becker's reconstruction, the oral stage of development represents that period of "primary narcissism" in which the child has not yet begun to differentiate its self from its primary caregivers. During the anal stage, the child begins to experience its self as separate from its caregivers and from its own body. That is, the body has become an object in the phenomenal field of the self. The child learns to understand that ego mastery of the body is the condition for continued closeness, affection, and care on the part of the caregivers. The child's narcissism extends to command and dominion of the object world through self-control (Becker 1973).

Finally, in the phallic stage, the child's ambivalence concerning this developmental process comes to full bloom in the awareness that parentally or socially prescribed symbolic meanings contain their own ego constrictions and sources of anxiety. There is but one solution to this dilemma of ambivalence: the child finally seeks to ground its ego in itself. The child seeks to become parent to itself. This is its lifelong project.

Having recast the Oedipus complex in this way, Becker went on to present castration fear and penis envy in the same light. Becker saw castration fear as centered primarily on the mother and not the father. The mother represents body pleasure and security. But at the same time the mother represents a primary and terrible threat to self-differentiation and the need to test one's personal powers in the object world. An incomparable comfort when one is hurt, scared, and in need of succor, the mother's love and protectiveness can be quicksand and dead weight when one is ready to explore and master the object world. The child has to be freed of her and the state of total dependency she represents.

The mother represents at this stage the world of the body, of inertia and animal determinism. While there is no denying the attraction of the mysteries, pleasures, and comforts of this world, the child has already learned that using the body as the primary vehicle for gaining self-esteem will not finally be tolerated in the adult world of symbolic meaning. The child has, so to speak, already been expelled from that paradise. The child's developing ego, to continue the metaphor, has already tasted the fruit of expansion through symbolic mastery of the object world. A total embrace of the body-meanings of the mother's world at this point could come only by complete capitulation of the child's ego to that of the mother. It would have to be totally on the mother's terms. The child would have to be removed of, castrated of, something that it now knows to be tangible, exciting, and real. This is the power and meaning of castration fears that arise in relation to the mother.

Penis envy is an existential complement to castration fear. Just as the mother appears to the child to be immersed in the world of the body—the world of breast milk, menstrual blood, and care for the physical needs of the family—so the father comes to represent freedom, movement, interaction, and mastery in the object world. The child cannot comprehend what the father does all day, but this only adds to the allure. The very absence of the father from the commonplace and daily routines of the household causes the child to associate the father with the great unknown, the outside world. As the child's developing ego seeks to test its powers of mastery in the object world, it is very comprehensible why it would gravitate toward a preference for the world of the father, while experiencing a need to reject and separate from the world of the mother. This is the power and meaning of penis envy in relation to the father.

By presenting the oedipal transition in transactional and existential terms, the social world of symbolic meaning replaced the instinct theory of human motivation. Becker was able to formulate a theory that also explained the implantation of the superego, of conscience, on a completely this-worldly basis, while avoiding the sexual reductionism of classical psychoanalysis. Because the child is seen as striving primarily for continued ego expansion within the context of continued support and affection of the caregivers, sex and sexuality become secondary and not primary motivational factors (Becker 1972).

There might appear to be anti-feminist leanings in this formulation. It must be kept in mind that Becker was writing more than a generation ago, when family roles were much more clearly defined and when feminist consciousness was only beginning to be raised. His specific formulation of these dynamics is admittedly dated and could easily be dismissed as the sputtering of patriarchy.

Becker assumed a model of the nuclear, heterosexual, two-parent family that too easily equated woman/mother/feminine with hearth and home and man/father/masculine with work outside the home. He was offering here a description and not a prescription. Furthermore, the fact that his formulations were constructed in direct dialogue with the categories of classical psychoanalysis made it even more difficult to shed the patriarchal overtones of the reference frame.

Becker recognized above all else that strictly defined social roles are a main cause of alienation in adult life. By recasting the Oedipus complex, castration anxiety, and penis envy in transactional and existential terms, he was able to demonstrate that both sexes confront these forces equally in the course of ego development. By extending the oedipal transition into adult life in the form of the oedipal project, he was able to demonstrate that these are forces that both sexes confront equally as adults. Furthermore, by being the main vehicle through which society offers its approval of individual striving and achievement, it is the strictly defined social role that, in effect, plays the part of arousing castration fear in adults. The more tightly defined the approved social role, the more personal ego expansion must be sacrificed in order to perform that role (Becker 1973).

There is no sense in trying to make a feminist out of Ernest Becker. However, a feminist reading of Becker is certainly possible. Becker pointed toward the ways in which individual personality growth is shaped, for better and for worse, by social arrangements. Becker assumed the traditional family structure in his recasting of the Oedipus complex. However, the transactional and existential dynamics he employed in this recasting are equally available for further adaptations to the wide variety of family structures toward which our society is moving.

Beyond the criticism that Becker assumed a traditional family structure in his writing, it could also be said that Becker's general view of the human being as an individual striving for mastery and recognition is itself descriptive of a male ego structure. The female ego structure might be quite different—for example, seeking cooperation and relationship rather than opposition, mutuality rather than personal gain, nurture of the other rather than naked self-interest. From this perspective we find in Becker simply one more example of a male theorist designating the male ego structure as human nature, and then judging the female ego structure by that measure.

There is certainly some validity to this criticism and it should be taken seriously, especially by those who would appeal to Becker's work in support of neoconservative political policies. However, it must be kept well in mind that in Becker's formulations, these so-called female personality traits are also easily understood as immortality strategies, shaped by the oedipal project in individual lives. As will be seen, in Becker's work there is no blanket denigration of female personality traits, nor any particular exultation of "male" personality traits. Both can be healthy and unhealthy. The assignment of gender to any personality characteristics is in any case a social construction.

The discussion continues between feminist theorists who suggest that women have deep-rooted differences in personality characteristics from men, and those feminists who claim that all perceived differences are a result of social environment. As women move into positions of traditional power in our society—in business, government, military—it remains to be seen whether genuine power transformations will result, or whether women will increasingly exhibit the same kind of behavior men in these positions have exhibited.

THE *CAUSA SUI* PROJECT

The oedipal project is the lifelong quest to become one's own parent, to find independent sources for grounding ego expansion. It is a striving for a self-grounded ego. Yet very few are able to establish their own meanings in an absolute sense and no one is able to sustain such personal meaning without interruption over time. Therefore, most people all of the time, and all people some of the time, must draw upon the established categories of culture for a personal sense of worth and forward movement. That sense of order and personal meaning imparted to individuals through participation in the wider society Becker (1973) refers to as the cultural *causa sui* project. It can be seen as an extension on the sociocultural level of the individual oedipal project.

Human beings are meaning-creating animals. Because this meaning always skates on thin ice above a lake of anxiety, it is very fragile and tentative. The creation and establishment of individual meaning is the defining urge of the expanding ego. To meet new experience in the world of objects with an adequate reservoir of skills that allow incorporation of that experience and confident action in relation to that experience is the very core of meaning. Self-esteem is maintained by the continued sense of meaning and purpose. Confident ability to act, self-esteem, feeling "right" in the world of objects, the sense of meaning and purpose—these become interconnected and even equivalent ways of speaking about mental health (Becker 1969). Blocks in the pathway present doubt and confusion. Continued blockage that cannot be reinterpreted and reconstituted begins the process of breakdown in mental health.

The ability to meet new experiences with confidence depends on a broad interpretive frame of reference, on a worldview, from which the person moves forward toward incorporation of the experience. Without this broad frame of reference, the ego has no mooring, no starting point, in the sea of experience. This broad frame of reference for meaning is what is supplied by the particular culture into which the person is socialized. The culture carries its own concrete images of truth—what is most important and is most highly valued.

Becker, drawing on Kluckhohn (1950), wrote of six basic human questions to which a viable culture gives answers: What is the relationship between human beings and nature? What is basic in human nature? What types of people are most valued? What are the basic modes of relating to others? What is the fundamental space/time dimension in which we live? What is my place in the hierarchy of power in nature and society? (Becker 1962b,c).

Cultural viability depends on providing convincing answers to these basic human questions. As anthropological studies have shown, cultural malaise and decline occur when people within a culture are no longer convinced of the truth of their received answers to these basic questions.[1]

---

1. Becker was most profoundly influenced not only by the anthropology faculty at Syracuse University and Sigmund Freud, but also especially by the works of Erving Goffman, John Dewey, Otto Rank, Norman O. Brown, and A. M. Hocart.

Looking at these questions more closely, we notice that they tell the person something very fundamental about both personal and social existence, namely, that there is an overall scheme of meaning in the universe into which individual and corporate life fit. That is to say that culture provides people with their sense of groundedness in the cosmos. Culture is what stands between human experience in the object world as potentially rational and meaningful and human experience in the object world as a chaotic jumble of sequential sense stimulations. Culture provides for human beings what instincts provide for bees, ants, and fish (Becker 1972).

The answers a particular culture provides to the basic questions of existence are self-referential. That is, if the question "How do we know?" is pursued, empirical inquiry (if that be the privileged epistemic method) must ultimately lead to myths, hagiography, and legends—that is, to other artifacts of the culture itself. What we see, then, is that the individual oedipal project—the project of establishing personal meaning—becomes grounded in the cultural *causa sui* project. Stated in terms of individual development, the cultural *causa sui* project is a direct extension of the oedipal project.

Presented in this perspective, a few other observations on the nature of culture are warranted. First, in relation to its answers to the most basic human questions, all cultures are sacred in character. This was seen also by Peter Homans (1989) who defined the sacred as "a series of diverse patterns of powerful, shared, and unconscious idealizations of esteemed cultural objects" (p. 19). On that deepest level, the distinction that Western culture makes between the sacred and the profane, or the religious and the secular, simply does not apply (Becker 1975).

Second, we can see why intensive cross-cultural contact is very threatening. Radically different answers are available to the basic human questions, each providing relatively satisfying answers, which give people confident grounding of their oedipal project in the cultural *causa sui*. Since there is no higher court of appeal to adjudicate between the truth of each, intensive cross-cultural contact tends to cast doubt on the transcendent and absolute nature of one's own cultural *causa sui*. This in turn places one's oedipal project in jeopardy, exposing one directly to the primal anxiety on which human personality is feebly built.

When cross-cultural contact is slow and takes place over many generations, the particular answers to the basic questions given in the contacting cultures have time to meld and unite, to the benefit of all concerned. But when the cross-cultural contact is quick and sudden—as when Western explorers barged in on the social pageantry taking place in the world outside of Europe—the doubts and anxieties can be overwhelming. Unfortunately, rather than contemplating the other's truth and reflecting on what it means for one's own sense of transcendence, it is much easier to deny and ridicule—or to make the next court of appeal whoever has the biggest guns. Now because of technology, especially rapid travel and communications, Europeans and Americans find themselves in the same position—living with doubt concerning the transcendent truth of their grand narrative—that they placed many people in other parts of the world in during the era of colonialism and imperialism. This doubt characterizes the postmodern consciousness.

A further observation was alluded to above, but it merits special remark because it is so important in Becker's thought. Becker, in fact, saw it as the very consensus of all social science. Human meaning in both the form of the individual oedipal project and in the form of the cultural *causa sui* is fundamentally fictional and arbitrary (Becker 1964b). It is a human construction that pretends to be more than that—it pretends to come from some transcendent source. To maintain the fiction of meaning, varying degrees of denial are necessary. Therefore, even the most viable of cultures carries within it the seeds of its own decadence and decline—directly analogous, one might say, to the individual psyche.

The very thing that characterizes postmodern consciousness is awareness of this fact, though we hardly know what to do with it. To characterize this consciousness, one thinks by way of analogy of the scene from *The Wizard of Oz* in which Toto pulled back the curtain to reveal a puny little man operating the awesome and transcendent wizard. The little man gave good advice—basically, look to your own powers for achieving your goals—but it is just not as convincing as having the same advice come from a terrible and awesome wizard.

From this we see why so-called fundamentalism is a uniquely modern phenomenon. Various stripes of cultural, political, and religious fundamentalists continue to deny that the curtain was ever opened and insist that their particular brand of meaning comes from the great wizard himself. But it is less and less convincing to contemporary human beings. The extra denial energy this fiction demands is bought at the price of ever-increasing isolation, alienation, and insulation from outsiders, or where available, by the use of instruments of coercion and violence. Such authoritarian moves are inherently expressive of anxiety concerning the viability of the particular frame of reference on the part of those making the appeal. For if the frame of reference were convincing in its own right, the coercive move would be unnecessary.

The cultural *causa sui* is arbitrary and fictional. It can only be maintained by varying degrees of denial. We look in envy at those of earlier times who could move easily from their personal oedipal project into the cultural *causa sui* and never feel the least pang of doubt. To them (we imagine) human existence was transcendently grounded and the individual served and participated in that transcendence simply by acting out the duties and tasks of expected cultural performance in whatever station the person happened to be born. How easy and natural life was "back then"!

Our nostalgic musings about the good old days are themselves largely fictional. Even a culture in its ascendant phase is based on the energy of denial and therefore contains within itself the very cultural contradictions that have always led to decadence and decline. Yet there is an extra dose of anxiety that those of postmodern consciousness must endure. The personal burden of anxiety in postmodernism stems from the fact that, even when compared with those who lived during a period of cultural decadence and decline, we know why our frantic offerings to the gods are no longer effective. Postmodern consciousness is one characterized by visible anxiety, as is borne out daily in the counselor's office.

This revealing of ourselves to ourselves, which Becker thought reached an entirely new plateau in Freud's outline of the Oedipus complex, is the most anxiety-arousing step that human beings can take (Becker 1972). Most people will pefer the comfort of any number of mundane diversions to keep from facing it.

Becker saw this knowledge concerning the fictitious and arbitrary nature of our meaning systems also as an opportunity, toward what he called the "second great step" in the evolution of consciousness. As was seen, the first step was the development of self through language (Becker 1964b). The second great step came with looking at the mechanisms of cultural transmission to understand how and in what ways we are reinstinctivized, thus allowing some measure of freedom in this process. But taking that second step is by no means automatically accomplished and until we figure out what to do with that information, even marginally reflective people must live under the burden of anxiety that it arouses. To a large extent, all kinds of counseling and therapies are, at their best, ways to help people face and cope with the anxiety this situation provokes. Or, at their worst, they are strategies to help people avoid and deny that anxiety. In his earlier writings, Becker was quite optimistic about the prospect of handling this anxiety. As he gained more understanding of the depth dynamics of human evil, his optimism was considerably tempered (Becker 1972).

THE URGE TO COSMIC HEROISM

Another major theme in Becker's thought now becomes intelligible. Each human being strives to maintain self-esteem through ego expansion in the world of objects. Self-esteem is predicated on seeing oneself and one's actions within a cultural worldview that gives satisfying answers to the basic human questions. One needs to place oneself within a frame of reference such that one's life makes sense not only in mundane terms but in transcendent terms. Each human being strives to be an object of primary value, a contributor to that which is transpersonal. Each person strives for nothing less than cosmic heroism (Becker 1972, 1973).

Put this bluntly, it may strike the reader as pathetically grandiose. One needs to see that in Becker's existential interpretive scheme of ego expansion, there are rather direct lines from early body mastery, to mastery in the object world, to self-esteem through meaning and purpose, to participation in transcendent immortality through the *causa sui*, to striving for cosmic heroism. All of these are simply ways of talking about the expansive side of the ego, and each has a corollary anxiety-based constriction as well.

The tendency to see even the everyday interactions of human beings in terms of the pompous and grandiose, of strutting and puffing, is a result of having seriously confronted the fictional character of all human meaning systems. If one person gains a sense of heroism, of adding to the transcendent cosmic scheme, by quietly working the fields and raising a family, while another must lead conquering armies out to subdue all within reach, each is nevertheless participating according to his or her station in the cultural *causa sui*, gaining thereby a particular sense of cosmic heroism (which is not to say you would be equally happy to have either as a next door neighbor).

The cultural *causa sui* project is basically a project for allowing people to gain a sense of cosmic heroism through adequate performance of their social role within the hierarchy of social power (Becker 1972). The rules, mores, ideas, and customs of a particular culture are in effect conduits for heroism. Through this heroism the person contributes to the fuller meaning of the universe, even in the face of personal death. Culture and society testify to the significance of human life. Without that assurance of transcending significance, the expansive aspect of the ego begins to turn in on itself, resulting in depression and despair.

This is again a central problem for people who share in the postmodern consciousness. For once one has seen behind the wizard's curtain, has seen the fictitious nature of human meaning systems, it is very difficult to maintain the kind of conviction necessary for performance of the prescribed pageants of heroism within a culture. The only way to achieve a sense of heroism is within a cultural system of symbolic fiction. Yet once the fictitious nature of the system is revealed, a person is deprived of this sense of heroism. The payoff of playing the social role in gaining a sense of cosmic significance simply isn't there any more once the system has been experienced as fictional and arbitrary. It is no accident that our time has been called an age of despair. If indeed depression is a modern disease of the mind, this is why.

Becker suggested that the study of culture might be approached as a study of comparative hero systems. What mechanisms for heroism are provided for what segments of society in a given culture? And because, like the cultural *causa sui*, these hero systems are fictitious and arbitrary, further inquiry could be made concerning the costs, in blood and alienation, for maintaining particular hero schemes. Who benefits and who pays? This type of inquiry, in a nutshell, would be the social scientific synthesis of Freud and Marx.

Because cultural heroics are intimately tied to the *causa sui* and oedipal projects, Becker spoke of personality disorders in terms of "failed heroics" (Becker 1973). We will look more at this later. For now we will end this section with two uninterpreted quotes from Becker that help us to understand what he was driving at with this concept of heroism. Subjecting one's own heroics to critical scrutiny is basically what Becker meant by "getting over one's Oedipus."

[It is] not a matter of simple reflection about his early family life, or even bringing to consciousness some of the most distasteful events of his childhood, or least of all a hard, rational scrutiny of one's motives. It is . . . going through hell of a lonely and racking rebirth where one throws off the lendings of culture, the costumes that fit us for life's roles, the masks and panoplies of our standardized heroisms, to stand alone and nude facing the howling elements as . . . a trembling animal element, . . . the disintegration of the self-esteem that sustains one's character . . . The question of personality growth and change, if it is deep-going and authentic, is usually whether one will end in madness or suicide or whether one will, somehow, be able to marshal the strength to take the first few steps in a strange world. [Becker 1972, p. 146]

If you . . . want to understand directly what is driving your patient, ask yourself simply how he thinks of himself as a hero, what constitutes the framework of reference for his heroic strivings—or better, for the clinical case, why does he not feel heroic in his life? [p. 77]

HUMAN EVIL

We see that in Becker's presentation, human beings are an evolving species striving to grasp the meaning of the whole of existence from the vantage point of being but part of that existence. For accomplishing this task, language is the main tool, yet language itself is a human artifact whose origin is but dimly understood.

The human species shares in the evolutionary history of all past and present species. As physical beings, they share completely in nature's demand that a living species maintain sources of nourishment, protection from the elements, and a suitable environment for procreation.

The human species is physically quite weak and vulnerable. Yet because of its powers of observation and reasoning and the ability to learn new skills, it has successfully adapted to various environmental conditions. However, humans are relative newcomers here and the story of our success or failure is ours to complete. Will we as a species learn to contain the raging in our breast and create true community among ourselves and with our environment? Or will it finally be said that we are but one more of those curious species for whom the very characteristics that for a time allowed the species to flourish in the end brought about its own extinction?

As a social species, human beings are nurtured in particular social environments and internalize the values of that social grouping. Group values, in turn, emerge from the particular history and experience of the group. Group values, therefore, are social products and, as factors in social maintenance, are one important aspect of species survival strategy.[2] The material root of values held as transcendent is the extent that social values encapsulate the survival wisdom of particular social groups. But the human is more than a material being. Humans have powers of mind that extend far beyond what is necessary for mere survival. This mental overload is the source of human creativity and aesthetic and emotional sensitivity, and is expressed symbolically in the assertion that besides the physical body humans also possess a soul or spirit. To speak of the human soul or spirit is to speak of that aspect

---

2. Compare this use of "survival" values to that which Becker applied to "public logic" (Becker 1961b).

of human thought and experience that seems to transcend and fly above the material world. And so in our art, work, relationships, and communities humans seek to arrange the physical world such that it bears the human stamp, the imprint of human personality.

Closely related to the work of the human soul and spirit is the ability to love (Becker 1964b). Giving and receiving love is the zenith of human creativity. In love people most clearly experience themselves as a unity of body, soul, and spirit. It is through love that personal energies can be most positively directed, so that individual works of creativity are lifted up and invested with meaning and significance far beyond what a material analysis of those works could convey. It is from this that humans gain their sense of being special in the material world. There is no other species that seems to possess this ability for transcending creativity in love in any degree approaching that of human beings.

At the same time we know there is something terribly wrong with human beings as a species. For while other animals may kill out of instinct and for food, only human beings kill for the purely sadistic joy of the act. Other animals might dumbly stand by while a fellow suffers out of helplessness and lack of understanding. But only humans purposely and knowingly inflict suffering on their fellows and stare at that suffering in Mephistophelian fascination, anxious for more!

Human beings are a self-contradictory animal. In terms of mental abilities, humans are truly divine beings, transcendent and ethereal. Mentally they create new worlds or sit on the far side of the planets. Yet this divine and ethereal soul or spirit is entirely dependent on a weak and vulnerable physical body, which hungers, thirsts, defecates, ages, and finally dies, taking the soul and spirit with it into the abyss of death. (For the time being we are assuming that doctrines of the afterlife or psychic survival of the body are fictional defenses against the terror of annihilation.) Divine beings this vulnerable to negation! It is no wonder there is a raging whirlwind in the breast!

As a result, human beings spend most of their psychic energy in the creation of symbols of immortality that allow, at least momentarily, suppression from consciousness the fact of their mortal, animal nature (Becker 1973). Humans are, for all their mental abilities, fleeting and mortal, here today and gone tomorrow, "fallen," as many great religious traditions have said. But human symbolic meanings point toward that which is higher, solid, lasting, eternal, whole, heroic, and immortal. Human striving is toward, as Becker saw so clearly, a denial of species determinism, a denial of death.

As far as we know, humans are the only species that knows and understands the reality of death years before it happens. Some animals never seem to understand death, even as the predator pounces or the butcher's blade is poised for the kill. Other animals do seem to experience a kind of terror just prior to the mortal blow—that look of terror on an animal face has haunted each and every one of us! But humans are a species who must live with that furious terror, now simmering, now boiling, from early childhood until the day the death angel calls.

Taming the terror is quite literally the central human psychological task. Without some success in taming this terror, in suppressing it from immediate consciousness, a person would be psychotically stunned and unable to maintain forward momentum.

The mechanism for taming of the terror is the creation of symbols of immortality with which people can identify themselves and through which people vicariously participate in immortality. According to this basic insight concerning the nature of being human, all people want to endure and prosper and in some sense gain immortality. But knowledge of mortality condemns them to mask this fact and suppress awareness of it from consciousness. With this we begin to understand the source of evil in our world.

> The thing that makes man the most devastating animal that ever stuck his neck up into the sky is that he wants a stature and a destiny that is impossible for an animal; he wants an earth that is not an earth but a heaven, and the price for this kind of fanatic ambition is to make the earth an even more eager graveyard than it naturally is. [Becker 1975, p. 96]

Human beings create symbols to represent immortality, and then treat the symbol as the object itself. That is, they become attached to the symbol as a fetish (Becker 1973). For example, wealth, in the form of accumulated goods and services, is a natural symbol of more life, of immortality, as that which stands opposed to deprivation and starvation.[3] Money provides the power to command goods and services and the symbol of wealth might therefore take the form of an accumulation of money. However, the accumulation of money almost inexorably takes on a power of its own, a psychological investment that is all but disconnected to the accumulation of goods and services. It is pursued for its own sake as a fetish. A fetish is a narrowing down in our symbol picture that has become irrational. The accumulation of wealth in the form of goods and services, because it aids in

---

3. Becker wrote an extremely insightful chapter on wealth, "Money: The New Universal Immortality Ideology" (Becker 1975, pp. 73–90). He was heavily influenced by the chapter, "Filthy Lucre," in N. O. Brown (1959).

survival, can be seen as reasonable, although it would surely also have a reasonable satiation point as well. But the pursuit of money for its own sake has no rational satiation point, for more zeroes can always be added! There is a sacrificial element involved in this kind of fetishism. As with idolatry, that which has been constructed becomes a consuming focus for life, causing the person to miss the true richness of life's experience. Life becomes too narrow and constricted.

Some degree of narrowing down, of constricting, is necessary to human life, for there is simply too much possible experience to digest (Becker 1975). Sitting alone in one closed room, it would be impossible to take in all that is truly there to experience (though some studies suggest that we absorb more through the subconscious than most of us could ever imagine). If all possible perceptions—the clock ticking, the heart beating, the voice of every person speaking, street noises—were to register in our consciousness with equal intensity, life would obviously be impossible. Attention is focused on that which is important and only these things become conscious. Most of what is going on passes by without notice. Given the totality of possible experience in each moment, a mind unable to narrow down to this degree would be stunned by the multiplicity of life.

But how narrowly must we constrict and narrow our experience? A life too narrow is impaired. A landscape perceived only in terms of a prospective development site is crippling. A fellow human perceived only as a client, a consumer, or the possessor of desired sexual organs is debilitating. It is to miss even that fullness of life that we, with our limited capacities, are able to experience.

Evil has been symbolized in all societies in terms of

animality, death, and decay. Satan, evil personified, is pictured with animal characteristics, living in the place of the dead, which reeks of putrification and feces. Satan's surroundings are filled with skulls and bones, vipers, dirt, and filth, and Satan is totally immersed in the physical world of sexual lust.[4]

Evil comes to have a clear moral sense about it as well, for Satan becomes the arch foe of the Good, of God. Therefore, as God becomes identified with that which is supportive of community, society, and civilization, evil becomes opposition to God's will, as acting contrary to God's law, and as contrary to the good of society. Evil is wickedness, disorder, and chaos.

We oppose evil, and rightly so. Our aversion to evil is rooted in the attempt to defeat mortality. We oppose evil as we oppose death! (Becker 1975). But now we have come to the problem of evil from the other side. For evil results in our attempts to deny our mortal state—yet we oppose evil as we oppose death. This needs further investigation.

We rightly oppose evil. Few among us consciously embrace evil, and those who do we consider clinically pathological. The liberal humanist tradition is to that extent correct when it posits the innate goodness of human beings—normal people choose the good and oppose evil.

Reality, however, is too much for us to take in—we must narrow it down. Likewise, mortality is too much for us to oppose. So we unconsciously narrow down our struggle against mortality to a struggle against evil. Mor-

---

4. Vivid pictorial and literary dramatizations of personified evil across many cultures are found in P. Carus, *The History of the Devil and the Idea of Evil* (1969) and in the many works of Prof. Jeffrey B. Russell.

tality we cannot oppose—but lawbreakers, yes! There is nothing we can do finally to halt death. But this enemy we can annihilate!

The basic theory of evil in this perspective is intelligible and clear. In our opposition to evil, we must of necessity narrow down and focus on specific evils, which represent mortality. Our motives in this are good and it is certainly better that specific evils be opposed than that no evils are opposed, even if ultimately we cannot solve the enigma of death. However, our tendencies are to narrow too much in our focus, leading us to think that the evil we oppose is the ultimate evil and that all will be well if we can simply defeat and wipe out this one focus of evil before us.

This is especially dangerous when we consider another fetishist urge to which we are prone in our manufacture of symbols, that of scapegoating, of identifying our narrowly focused evil of evils with particular persons, groups, races, ideologies. Once that happens the natural identification or eradication of evil with God's cause insures that massacres will continue as sacramental acts! It becomes all but impossible to place limits on the violence we are willing to employ in fighting this evil. Thus the stage is set for the treacheries and demonic events of human history. Ironically, the worst of these atrocities, symbolized by Auschwitz and Hiroshima, were the actions of nations who have been considered by many to be beacons of reason and enlightenment in our world. In both cases, as later generations stand in those places where racial and nuclear holocausts have occurred, it is very difficult to even imagine what sort of evil these people thought they were confronting that would justify these means employed to fight against it.

We see, therefore, that in seeking to fight against evil, human beings bring ever more evil into the world, because all but inevitably the evil we fight against has been too narrowly defined and too narrowly focused on other human beings and ideologies.

> But if we add together the logic of the heroic struggle against evil with the necessary fetishization of evil, we get a formula that is no longer pathetic but terrifying. It explains almost by itself why man, of all animals, has caused the most devastation on earth—the most real evil. He struggles extra hard to be immune to death because he alone is conscious of it; but by being able to identify and isolate evil arbitrarily, he is capable of lashing out in all directions against imagined dangers of this world. . . . Man is an animal who must fetishize in order to survive and have "normal mental health." But this shrinkage of vision that permits him to survive also at the same time prevents him from having the overall understanding he needs to plan for and control the effects of his shrinkage of experience. [Becker 1973, pp. 150, 153]

This is why human evil in Becker's presentation is so ambiguous and so frightening. Humans commit evil acts out of heroic intentions, the very desire to eradicate evil. It is no wonder that the generals on both sides of any conflict see themselves as working toward the good, fighting evil, and able to repeat with fullest conviction, "God is with us!" When we examine ourselves and others, what we find is not an immediate desire to slay, maim, hurt, and kill (or if so, we rightly consider the person clinically pathological). What we find is the intention to struggle heroically against evil! Human beings will identify willy-nilly as "enemy" that which potentially threatens personal expansion or that of the group, images of evil that are culturally transmitted and over which the individual has little control.

4

Transference and Terror

*Everyone needs protection
from what they don't know.*

S. J. Marks

PSYCHOANALYTIC TRANSFERENCE

What makes people act the way they do? Ernest Becker approached this question both in terms of individual actions and in terms of group behavior. He saw that the two were closely related, leading him to a deeper understanding of transference (Becker 1973).

Transference in psychoanalytic literature generally refers to the very strong emotions of the client toward the counselor that emerge in the course of therapy (Laplanche and Pontalis 1973). These may be either strongly negative emotions or strongly positive emotions. It is assumed in psychoanalysis that strong negative emotions are based on unresolved childhood conflicts in which the client transfers the anger, hatred, and ambivalence experienced during that period of life onto the therapist. The emergence of strong negative transference can then be used by the therapist to uncover these unresolved conflicts of the past and, by working through these feelings with the therapist, the client can be helped to resolve the conflicts in the unconscious.

Clinicians are also well aware of the fact that clients will form very intense and clinging attachments to the therapist. The therapist is experienced by the client as an all-wise, all-knowing, and even all-powerful being and the client magnifies the personal qualities of the therapist beyond any sense of proportion (Giovacchini 1987).

While this kind of positive transference is less valuable for therapy and can place an enormous moral strain on the therapist, it happens with consistent regularity. This fact intrigued Freud, who theorized that humans carry within themselves a strong desire for passive and dependent protection, based in the childhood experience of dependence on parental caregivers. This desire is transferred to the therapist in the course of analysis, causing the patient to view the therapist in the same light of omnipotence with which the child experienced its adult caregivers.

Freud theorized that this desire was the basis for the trance state in hypnosis, as well as the reason why, especially in groups, people will so willingly submit to authoritarian leaders and leadership structures (Freud 1921). That the submission can be total was evidence for Freud that it was erotic in nature and rooted in infantile sexual desire directed toward the parental objects. This view was developed further by other contributors to the psychoanalytic corpus.

Becker was very appreciative of Freud's interpretation on this issue and considered it "the key to a universal underlying historical psychology" (Becker 1973, p.131).

Becker saw that this theory explained most clearly why people engage in acts of sadism in a group context that they would never even consider in another situation and for which they might later be shocked and ashamed. For if the leader comes to represent the omnipotent parent, the person wants nothing more than to submit and serve. Since it is the parents who, during the oedipal transition process, facilitate the development of the superego, a conscience, a sense of right and wrong, then an authoritarian leader acting in that role can override the constrictions of the superego and sanction any sort of behavior in its place.

Becker considered this an important fact about human beings that was already tacitly suggested by Freud. Reality reveals to us the fact that as individual people, we are finite, mortal, weak animals. Given the choice between accepting this reality or giving oneself over to illusions of greatness and importance that the leader imparts to followers, the mass of human beings will choose illusion over reality, lies over truth, fiction over fact and will strike out in holy rage against anyone or anything that threatens to shatter the illusion to which they have committed themselves (Becker 1975). This is the nature of the bond between leader and follower, between individual and group behavior. It is a bond rooted in the regressive transference of individual submission to power, in the individual need to feel awe and protection from the symbolic icons of power by which the person can deny and avoid recognition of finitude. Furthermore, people do not simply find themselves passively engulfed by such feelings toward symbolic icons of power. People actively and all but consciously seek such symbolic icons of powers toward which they might submit themselves, even when, perhaps even especially when, this is done under the ideological cover of seeking independence, individuation, self-actualization, self-fulfill-ment, and autonomy. We will return to this in our later discussion of the limits of psychotherapy.

THE LEADER AND THE GROUP

The leader imparts to the group members a sense of transcendent expansion, sanction for sadistic or licentious behavior, and group cohesiveness based on the dynamic of regressive transference (Becker 1973). The leader offers the group opportunity to maintain the illusion of power in the face of ontological finitude. The leader does this by assuming the burden of guilt for the concrete actions of the group members as well as the existential guilt of "being" for the group. The price each person pays for this service is obedience to the authority of the leader.

The very power of the leader is the source of his or her vulnerability as well. The relationship between the leader and the group is not simply unidirectional. Looked at from the other side, the leader is created by the group. While there are natural leadership qualities that will make a certain individual seem to be a "born leader," the specifics of these qualities vary widely from culture to culture. It is the group that recognizes and responds to these qualities of leadership exhibited and embodied in particular individuals.

Another way of viewing the leader/group relationship is to see the group members as actively and all but consciously in search of people who, by the specific outlines of their particular cultural hero system, embody and exhibit those qualities of leadership required by the group members for the successful functioning of their regressive transference. When the group finds such a person (perhaps after some sequence of trial and error) the members are more than willing to surrender their will to that of the leader.

In this surrender, very strong and specific demands are placed on the leader to fulfill the expected role that the group requires for regressive transference. Contrary to the mythological constructs of the hero systems of numerous cultures, even the most exalted and powerful of human leaders are human beings and not gods. The group holds as firm a grip on the leader as the leader holds on the group. They hold the leader hostage to the expectations of the group, and the group will not hesitate to move against a leader who ceases to exhibit this ability to lead!

Building on the insights of Freud and others concerning transference and group behavior, Becker (1973) suggested that this transference dynamic is present in all human behavior. Transference is not simply neurotic behavior but normal behavior. Or better said, normal behavior is neurotic behavior. Human behavior can best be interpreted as a continuum of strengths and weaknesses, with no hard-and-fast lines of demarcation between what is normal and what is neurotic. If we view neurosis as a continuum, however, we have to become aware of those features of ourselves that we would rather pretend do not exist. Seen in this light, there is no convincing philosophical or therapeutic justification for the division between "healers" and "sick," between "we" and "them," which the medical model of psychiatry implies. This theme, which is being echoed in the current literature (Goldstein 1990b), began to dominate Becker's mature work.

What Becker saw is that human destructiveness is not simply a matter of acquisitive appetites out of control, material conflicts of interest, or clumsy ignorance of sophisticated conflict resolution methods. Human destructiveness is rooted in the ontological fact of human finitude on the one hand and on the other hand the very real human need for illusions, lies, and fictions concerning this fact of ontology. Experience, education, material equality, and conflict mediation will lessen the frequency with which humans resort to overt institutions of violence such as organized warfare. This is to be encouraged at every point. Yet Becker began to understand that at its deepest levels, human resort to violence is rooted in an existential urge to deny and avoid ontological finitude. That is a different problem altogether from the subject matter of professional peace studies.

TRANSFERENCE AND NORMALITY

Freud theorized that the human desire to submit to authority is rooted in sexual motivation. Becker recast this in an existential/ontological direction. Becker sought to ground his views in the general human condition rather than in specific erotic drives. This allowed his theories to mutually influence the emerging interdisciplinary consensus concerning the fictional nature of human meaning systems and the plasticity of human character. According to Becker, transference is motivated by a real terror of both life and death. As he wrote,

> people seek merger with the parental omnipotence not out of desire but out of cowardice . . . The fact that transference could lead to complete subjection proves not its "erotic character" but something quite different: its "truthful" character, we might say. . . . it is the immortality motive and not the sexual one that must bear the larger burden of our explanation of human passion. [Becker 1973, p. 142]

In his mature theory of human motivation, Becker pointed toward two ontological drives—the fear of death and the fear of life. He found a definite cowardliness, dread, and fear of both life and death on the one hand and on the other hand a definite attraction toward heroism, goodness, beauty, and perfection.

The attraction toward heroism Becker located in the human conscience. This desire to do what is right and to feel good is an extension of what Becker earlier had summarized in the concept of self-esteem. Each person has an aesthetic urge toward perfection and wholeness that is an integral component of self-esteem. Each person's sense of perfection is shaped by culture and upbringing. Within one culture, normally socialized people tend to share basic notions, with variations occurring due to individual experiences.

While other species (if we may speak anthropomorphically) also seem to desire to feel good by living expansively in the environment according to their nature and instincts, human beings cannot easily do this. Having exchanged instinctual meaning for symbolic meaning in the course of evolution, human beings no longer have a clear and unambiguous nature by which to live in the world. Animals need not contemplate just what truth, goodness, and beauty mean for them. For human beings this is a primary activity, sometimes even prior to basic bodily care. The reason for this is that while humans do want to merge with oceanic nature, at the same time there is an equally strong urge to stand out from nature as something unique in the universe. To deny, neglect, or ignore either pole in human beings can only be done by concerted repression of that which is basic to human character.

Is it possible to reconcile these two poles of being human? That is finally the problem of psychotherapy and the point at which therapy and spirituality meet. Putting the dilemma in this light allows us yet another handle on what Becker meant by transference. Transference, in a nutshell, is the dynamic of drawing personal symbolic power from external sources. Transference is the psychological mechanism by which an individual feels grounded in the object world and at the same time feels powerful, important, and unique—standing, as it were, above nature. Because of the need to feel powerful, important, and unique, normally socialized people choose a combination of transference objects that symbolize strength, power, or beauty to the majority of people living in their particular culture. In American culture in the late twentieth century, for example, transference objects like the flag, money, cars, famous people, and so on are easily understood, if not shared, by the majority of people. Transference objects such as specialized collections, technical gadgets, a romantic or intellectual interest, a club, association, or social movement are shared by fewer people, yet well understood by the majority. They are considered safely normal, if perhaps idiosyncratic—so long as one is not fanatical about one peculiar transference object (that is, has a combination of transference objects that are shared by many other people).

In Becker's presentation, transference links even a perversion like fetishism to the same inner motives that we find in everyday normal living. As he wrote,

> transference is a form of fetishism, a form of narrow control that anchors our own problems. We take our helplessness, our guilt, our conflicts, and we fix them to a spot in the environment. We can create any locus

> at all for projecting our cares onto the world, even the
> locus of our own arms and legs. [Becker 1973, p. 144]

Because humans are symbolic creatures and can arbi-
trarily invest any concept or object with talismanic power,
there is nothing that limits our choice of transference
objects to that which the majority prefer or approve.
Perhaps I find a crystal or rabbit foot worn next to my body
gives me power, groundedness, potency. Perhaps this and
nothing else yields feelings of power, no combinations. I
am totally fixed on this one transference object. Perhaps it
is a shoe, a piece of underclothing . . .

In Becker's view, people use transference as a way of
dealing with the real terror of feeling powerless, ungroun-
ded, weak, and alone—the very feelings that, because of
the development of an individualized ego and personality
in human beings, must be shouldered by the human
species alone. The first transference object in the lives of
most people is probably their parents or caregivers. But as
the ability to symbolize develops, the child soon learns that
almost any object will suffice if necessary, such as a teddy
bear or blanket. We symbolically invest a particular transference object with power to protect and reassure us of our
place in the universe.

The ambivalence felt toward both positive and negative transference objects is based on this investment of
power. As Becker wrote,

> In some complex ways the child has to fight against
> the power of the parents in their awesome miraculous-
> ness . . . Now we see why the transference object poses
> so many problems. The child does partly control his
> larger fate by it, but it becomes his new fate. He binds
> himself to one person to automatically control terror,
> to mediate wonder, and to defeat death by that per-

son's strength. But then he experiences "transference
terror"; the terror of losing the object, of displeasing it,
of not being able to live without it. The terror of his
own finitude and impotence still haunts him, but now
in the precise form of the transference object. [Becker
1973, p. 146]

In Becker's view, transference dynamics pervade all
of human life and are inseparable from the ontological fact
of our human condition. Transference dynamics lay at the
root of much human misery, oppression, and bamboozle-
ment. Yet for an animal who has raised its head with the
new gift of self-consciousness and, surveying the universe,
finds itself alone, threatened on every side and awaiting
the finality of death, life without some form of transference
would be unbearable. Without transference of any kind, we
would simply be psychotically stunned every time we
lifted our minds from total absorption in all but the most
mundane of occupations.

Transference is also the root of our urge toward the
heroic, toward truth, beauty, and goodness. But this is not
the whole story. Becker (1973) wrote, "What makes transcendence heroics demeaning is that the process is unconscious and reflexive, not fully in one's control" (p. 156).
The tragedy of transference dynamics is that our transference objects are mediated to us without our conscious
control or reflective input. If we were able to exercise some
thoughtful control and judgment in choosing our transference objects, the negative side effects would be greatly
reduced.

TRANSFERENCE AND IDOLATRY

The analogy of this presentation of transference to the
ancient Israelite struggle against idolatry is instructive

here. Idol worship is the most explicit example of transference dynamics and the idol is the most explicit example of a transference object. In the most advanced societies of the ancient world, there were complex hierarchies of idols and the powers these idols represented, from the central idol of the national or city-state political system, ranged from the powers of political control down to the household idols' powers of individual families and their place in the overall system of order and control.

Idols are made by human hands and initially only represent external powers in the environment. But once the idols were constructed and psychologically invested with power through transference dynamics, these objects of wood, stone, and metal took on power significance in their own right. They became the central focus for people's lives and behaviorally had real power over the existence of the people. We might see this psychoanalytically as a process of transitional objects coming to replace the primary object itself.

The ancient Israelites did not deny the existence of external powers that governed and ordered the universe. But they experienced the dark side of the cultural hero system of monarchy in their very bodies, in Egyptian bondage for some tribes and in the heavy burden of taxes, coerced labor, and other forms of exploitation of agricultural communities by the city-states for other tribes (Gottwald 1979). The maintenance of any social fiction has an underside, a shadow side, and demands victims. Having experienced this underside of the system in their own persons, these people were united by their determination to reject the power transference dynamics of their environment.

Although it was certainly not uniform among them at all times, the genius of ancient Israelite ideology was their rejection of idols as legitimate transference objects, as the legitimate focus for the ordering of their communal life. What was the point in this? If there was a recognition of powers, what harm could there be in locating those powers in specific objects? Was it just simple stubbornness that caused the ancient Israelites to abhor so strongly the complex system of idol worship of their neighbors?

The fact is that if Moloch, Marduk, Osiris, Baal, or the Pharaoh only made the crops grow and brought peace and prosperity, it would be difficult to criticize the particular cultic manifestation of the culture that produced them. But the price paid for this social fiction of idol worship was always a combination of heavy tax burdens, conscription for labor and war, and human sacrifice.

The people of the ancient Near East were very accepting of a multiplicity of powers and the representation of these powers in a plethora of idols. But it was simply incomprehensible that a people would choose "no-thing" as a transference object for the focus of these powers. A god that had no representation in a concrete transference object—an idol—was literally "no thing" to these people. A tribal union based on the worship of no-thing must have struck them as not just impious and inferior, but downright crazy behavior.

The central issue between the ancient Israelites and their neighbors was not whether there was a God, but rather what kind of God it was. To maintain a system of worship of a God who could not be focused in a concrete transference object (and therefore be controlled by the cultic system) placed a great burden of anxiety on the people, as can be seen clearly especially in those biblical passages relating to the controversy surrounding the establishment of kingship among the ancient Israelites. In actual practice the ancient Israelites also set up transference objects, in the form of special altars, the use of minor idols, and finally the political institution of kingship as a focus for the power of their God. But through the institution of the prophets, periodic cleansing of these idolatrous encroachments were carried out in the name of a transference object, *YHWH*, which could not be controlled by the people (I-will-be-what-I-will-be) and would demand of the people social justice rather than cultic sacrifice.

In relation to this central issue, these dynamics were repeated in the early Christian encounter with Roman emperor worship. These early Christians were perceived by the Romans as not just impious, but crazy and even atheistic (Wilken 1984).

With this historical analogy in mind, let us return to the problem of transference dynamics in the modern world. The problem with transference dynamics is not in the process itself, but rather in the fact that our transference objects are selected reflexively, without intelligent control or any awareness of the underside, the shadow side, the price that must be paid for making any particular transference object the locus for ordering our lives.

Psychotherapy can be seen as the process of helping the client make conscious the transference objects by which he or she is ordering life and gaining a sense of protection and structure in the world and the price that the person pays for the selection of these particular transference objects (Becker 1973). These transference objects may be very concrete and inanimate, such as a car, a house, a job, or they may be such things as social and parental voices of the superego concerning family roles, proper behavior, and so on. For the most part, the person has already found the underside, the shadow side, to be dysfunctional. The price paid in the form of stress, broken relationships, and phobias is too high, for that is why the person sought therapy in the first place. By bringing the unconscious choices of transference objects into the conscious awareness of the client, the client is enabled to make thoughtful changes. The client is enabled to take some control in the selection of transference objects and make some reflective decisions concerning what transference objects are best suited to the reality of the client's life situation.

The process is not simply intellectual and an easy matter of insight alone. These transference objects are what psychologically allow the ego to feel grounded, secure, safe. To recognize the fictional nature of these objects casts the ego into chaos. The psychotherapist must expect a process of constant resistance to having these sources of power revealed. The psychological depth of this dilemma for the client is the topic of discussion in the next chapter.

In conclusion, let it be stressed that Becker's presentation of transference dynamics and transference objects, seen as analogous to the ancient Israelite and early Christian struggle against idol worship, brings our understanding of the commonalities between psychotherapy and pastoral counseling to a point of agreement voiced by numerous writers. While the differences between the psychotherapeutic and the religious approaches to counseling must be respected, they share the common aim of freeing people from attachment to idols. In other words, if these approaches disagree on what God is, they certainly agree on what God is not!

5

Death and the Limits
of Psychotherapy

*You're inside something you can't find a way out of,
you're ready now to hear what
you should.*

S. J. Marks

DEATH AND REPRESSION

Why do people act the way they do? By the time Ernest Becker wrote his mature works, he began to see that a well-rounded, interdisciplinary, and empirical/scientific picture of the human condition would have to take some rather unexpected turns. He began to understand that even mundane, everyday actions grow out of an acutely existential and ontological dilemma. A symbol-creating animal must mask anxieties of finitude and numb itself to its own precariousness in the face of threats of abandonment and annihilation. For such a being, even mundane events can take on the character of life and death (Becker 1973).

Consciousness of self, the paramount human characteristic, necessarily entails consciousness and knowledge of death. In Becker's understanding of human motivation, awareness of death, the anxiety that this provokes, and the strategies people devise to deal with the anxiety are at the very core of why we act the way we do.

It would be too naive just to say that we are motivated by the fear of death. That simple formula is easily countered by examples of people who, in situations of extremity, have willingly chosen death. Furthermore, people engage regularly in behaviors such as smoking or driving a car, which, if anything, would indicate that fear of death is the farthest thing from their minds. To understand what Becker was saying by this, we need to approach death not as the concrete, bodily bluntness of dead corpses but rather as a very complex psychological symbol.

Death anxiety is not present in young children, who have no clear understanding of death.[1] The infant strives to thrive and grow on an organismic level and to experience warmth and care on the psychological level. Being totally dependent on its caregivers for this, the first anxiety a child experiences is that of abandonment. This is only indirectly a death anxiety and is not experienced as such by the child. Death anxiety is not the basic anxiety if that is determined by chronological priority. But existentially, it is possible to see that first anxieties are not necessarily the basic anxieties in psychologically developed adults. By the time one is able to comprehend the sequence of object loss = inability to thrive = death, we may assume that death anxiety, dread of annihilation, has already

---

1. The fear of death is traced through life stages in J. Meyer's *Death and Neurosis* (1975). I find in Meyer's work, which was written in Germany at the same time Becker was writing his last works, an independent and clinical confirmation of the main points concerning the fear of death that Becker presented.

superseded mere abandonment as the basic anxiety. That is to say that as the self becomes an object of consciousness, the anxiety of object loss becomes the anxiety of loss of self. In Becker's (1973) view, death as a symbol summarizes the entire spectrum of adult anxiety.

If fear of death is the basic anxiety of adults, why are so few aware of it? Becker's answer to this was repression. Fundamental repression is not directed toward instinctual libidinal drives but toward the basic human condition. It is not a simple and straightforward negation. Becker understood repression as an essential and creative force of the ego used to further ego enhancement. Because death is an inescapable fact of our animal nature, fear of death is natural and inevitable to any animal who has gained a sense of self-consciousness. Yet to live in a state of immediate consciousness of death would be to live in constant panic, dread, and paralysis. The forward movement of living would be severely impaired, as happens in cases of psychosis. Repression serves the interest of the ego in blocking from immediate awareness the consciousness of death, thus allowing normal life to continue.

Immediately we face a major paradox of human existence in this formulation. Death is a fact for all human beings. There is no escape from it and it could happen at any moment. Yet those who are most realistic and unrepressed, people for whom this awareness is right on the surface, are those least able to act. Likewise, those who are most able to act with equanimity and ease are those who are the most repressed and oblivious to this basic reality. Repression in Becker's view is more positive than negative. Only half tongue-in-cheek did Becker take a poke at the human-potential movement in suggesting that a really repression-free existence would resemble schizophrenia.

Yet repression is not a one-dimensional positive phenomenon. The real human condition must strike sheer terror in the heart of anyone who faces it head on. That we are both divine beings and food for worms is too much to psychologically digest. If the ego uses repression in order to maintain normal mental health, there is a price to be paid. There is always the return of the repressed. Becker poignantly summed up the genius of psychoanalysis in suggesting that it "revealed to us the complex penalties of denying the truth of man's condition, what we might call the costs of pretending not to be mad" (Becker 1973, p. 29).

What Becker was saying is that while on the one hand repression allows normal living to proceed, it does so only by closing the doors of perception to much that is undeniably real about human existence. The price paid for keeping our psyche from being continually flooded with the real terror of the human situation is shrinkage of experience, a preference for habitual perceptions and responses and a narrowing down of our ability to see alternative points of view and alternative responses.

Becker suggested that what in the literature of psychoanalysis is referred to as specific character types can easily be understood as broad groupings of habitually preferred ways of perceiving and responding in the context of this shrinkage of experience. Character type varies according to the specific circumstances of individual upbringing. Because of its commitment to the theory of libidinal sexual drives as the foundation for character, psychoanalysis grouped these character types around specific erogenous zones—oral, anal, and phallic. In Becker's recasting of the basis for character formation, the use of erogenous zones to designate groupings continues to make sense. But not because of the libidinal drive theory, which has been largely abandoned in social science. It continues to makes sense because in specific families and individual circumstances of upbringing, early training during the oedipal transition phase is likely to give an extra charge of anxiety to the learning around one of these bodily orifices. As the child picks up on that extra charge of anxiety that within its particular family group is associated with particular body parts and body functions, the child's habitual repressive preferences begin to be formed. The learning of specific styles of habitual repressive preferences is essentially what Becker meant by character formation (Becker 1962b).

Narrowing down of experience in repression, learning of habitual repressive preferences, and refusal or even inability to perceive the fullness of a situation and to formulate alternative responses are all ways of speaking about the price we pay for protecting ourselves from being flooded by overwhelming anxiety in the face of the real terror of the human situation. Becker referred to all of this collectively as "character armor," a term he borrowed from Reich (1970). Becker expanded on it in an especially vivid way to describe the human being as the "angel in armor," the divine being who must protect itself against normal, everyday life (Becker 1969). "Character armor" is a very apt phrase that highlights the ambiguity of human existence. The metal armor worn by the knights of old protected the person inside against the onslaught of enemy blows and arrows. But at the same time it severely restricted the person's range of vision and scope of movement. The suit of armor was of value in one arena and one arena only.

Character armor also protects the ego from overwhelming anxiety. But just as it protects, so also does it severely restrict. Arguably functional and necessary within the arena in which it was formed, it may be very dysfunctional in new and different circumstances. The person's habitual repressive preferences inform one that what is happening now is like what has happened before. This may prevent the person from seeing new situations for what they really are.

This we all do. We could not live and function without character armor. Without it we would be faced with a continual onslaught of overwhelming anxiety, an anxiety rooted in the terror of abandonment, loneliness, finitude, animality, exposure, and unprotectedness, of the void of nothingness, of nonbeing—the terror of death. The prospect we face in personal growth, therefore, is not one of living in the absence of character armor. Our character armor forms who we are as individuals. But how much repression is necessary? How protected must we be? When habitual perceptions and responses have become clearly dysfunctional in new situations, causing us to hurt and damage people we love, or always to miss out on creative and joyful experiences, can we shed at least some of that armor?

This is the question we face in personal growth and in therapy. Our character armor was formed reflexively, without our knowing what was happening to us. It was formed by our family situation, by the particulars of our upbringing, by the particulars of class, cultural, and social prejudices to which we have been exposed. It was formed without our conscious consent, so to speak. By making our habitual repressive responses, our character armor, an object of conscious awareness, it might be possible to take at least some conscious control and shed the part of it that is most severely blocking us at a particular point in time.

The process of making our character armor an object of our consciousness and taking some rational control of it is the very process of personal growth and of therapy. But it is also a process that exposes the ego to the very anxiety from which the armor was designed to protect it. A decision to look at our armor full in the face, to see and understand how and why it was formed, is by its very nature a decision to face the anxiety of finitude, the terror of death. The promise of therapy is a greater ability to adjust, to love, and to experience creativity and joy. But the lake of anxiety from which our character armor protects us also defines the limits of therapy.

THE LIMITS OF THERAPY

Once we have looked at the problem of human existence from the perspective that Becker presented, it becomes very clear that what is wrong with human life is the fact of life itself—that we are born to die (Becker 1973). There is simply no therapy that will answer the real and root cause of anxiety. There is no therapy or strategy for personal growth that can give people what they really want, which is immortality. The human condition is finally one of agony, tragedy, despair, and death. And the more self-actualized or liberated the individual becomes, the more that individual is brought face to face with this reality. As Becker (1973) wrote,

> The person is stuck with the full problem of himself, and yet he cannot rely on himself to make any sense out of it . . . What does it mean, then . . . to talk such fine-sounding phrases like "Being cognition," "the fully centered person," "full humanism," "the joy of peak experiences," or whatever, unless we seriously qualify such ideas with the burden and the dread that they also carry? . . . we must remember that life itself is the insurmountable problem. [pp. 269–270]

Faced with the dread and burden of life itself, people gain their strength, their sense of security and protection, from others. As we saw, this dynamic of gaining strength from others, which begins in earliest childhood as the child gains its sense of security and protection from its care-givers, is the dynamic of transference. What people seek from the outside is what Becker called an "immortality ideology" (Becker 1975, p. 5), in which to find security and protection. By giving allegiance to some external source of symbolic power, whether in the form of a particular per-son, the cultural *causa sui* project, a political group or movement, or in abject idol worship, the anxieties of personal finitude are calmed and kept at bay.

Counseling and therapy can help people who are particularly twisted and hemmed in by their habitual repressive preferences. It can help those so motivated to become consciously aware of the immortality ideologies to which they have given allegiance in the past, along with the consequences this has had in their lives. It can help those so motivated to look at the underside, the unin-tended consequences, the price that is paid for giving their devotion and loyalty to particular sources of security and protection. In this way the person can be aided in taking some intelligent control of what have been reflexive and unconscious motivations in that person's life. Yet if Becker (and here Becker, who was open about his indebtedness to Otto Rank, followed closely Rank's [1958] formulations) was correct, this is not finally what people want. They want a new immortality ideology. They want religion. Honest psychology simply cannot deliver on that desire.

Many approaches to therapy and counseling in our time have tried to answer this human need by making of psychology or psychotherapy itself a new immortality ideology. Becker (1972) saw this happening on various levels that are continuing in the present.

The first way that psychology becomes a new immortality ideology is limited to the few, such as Freud, who developed totalistic explanatory systems and used those systems as personal immortality ideologies (Becker 1973). The closest disciples of such people may also participate in and perpetuate the aura of power that the system generates. By nearly exclusive use of the language and symbols of a particular system in everyday life, the system becomes, in effect, a living system of belief. The countertransference dynamics involved in maintaining such an immortality ideology might include aloofness or disdain for the unenlightened outside the fold, rejection and excommunication of dissenters within the fold, narrowness of perception in an attempt to make all new experiences fit the system, and endless arguments and divisions over the fine points of officially sanctioned interpretations. All allegiances to human products as symbols of immortality power have an underside and exact a price.

Another way that psychology becomes a new immortality ideology is to supplement it with explicitly metaphysical doctrines and teachings. Much of the New Age therapies and recovery programs we see in our time clearly move in this direction. Becker saw the power of such approaches as coming from the religious nature of the doctrines. But he also saw in some of these therapies that the power source was rooted in the transference dynamics of the person of the guru-psychologist. Of such Becker (1973) wrote,

> the psychotherapist himself beams out the steady and quiet power of transference and becomes the guru-

figure of the religion. No wonder we are seeing such a proliferation of psychological gurus in our time. It is the perfect and logical development of the fetishization of psychology as a belief system. It extends that system into its necessary dimension, which is immortality and the life-enhancing power that goes with it. [p. 273]

Becker saw that in such therapies, there is usually a studied disregard for examination of transference and countertransference dynamics. After all, such an examination could only expose the clay feet of the system itself. By ignoring transference and countertransference dynamics in these therapies,

> the aura of guru infallibility remains intact and provides an automatic shelter for the patient's deep yearnings for safety and security. It is no accident, either, that the therapists who practice these guru therapies cultivate themselves with halo-like beards and hairdos, to look the part they play. [p. 273]

Honest pastoral and psychological counseling and therapy can play a positive role in helping people to live lives that are less reflexive and compulsive, less restricted, less damaging to others, lives with enhanced possibilities for creativity, joy, and spiritual depth. But honest counselors and therapists must also be clear that this is achieved only when the patient assumes the burden of increased anxiety.

There is a dark night of the soul[2] attached to personal

---

2. The dark night of the soul is a very old image associated with the European mystical tradition, especially with St. John of the Cross. Harkness (1945) places this image in a modern spiritual and psychological context.

growth. The work of the patient in therapy is to confront and shoulder this increased burden of anxiety. It takes an enormous amount of ego strength to shoulder this burden. A therapist must be clear about the costs as well as the benefits of therapy, about the possibilities as well as the limitations. If the root problem of life is life itself, then those therapies that offer joy without pain, growth without suffering, and unlimited potentialities for living must be seen as extremely problematic.

6

Metaxy— Life In-Between: A Model of Adult Psychology

*You always stretch the limits,
to see how close you can go to death and still be alive
how much you can dare as a human
without killing yourself.*

S. J. Marks

THE ONTOLOGICAL AXIS

What makes people act the way they do? By the time Ernest Becker wrote his mature works, he was deeply committed to an existentialist frame of reference for understanding human behavior, a frame of reference that rejected an Aristotelian model of homeostasis in favor of a model of the dynamic movement of balance. What makes this commitment so intriguing is the fact that Becker did not bring this frame of reference to his work as a prior philosophical doctrine. He began as an empirical social scientist, an empirical phenomenologist, with a firm grounding in anthropology, sociology, and psychoanalysis. He was drawn to the existentialist framework by following his empiricist method to its conclusion. Explicitly existentialist views took shape slowly and began to appear rather late in his writing.

Becker's mature model of adult psychology views human existence as standing between ontological pulls on the one hand and existential pulls on the other. (See Figure 6–1.) He characterized the ontological axis as the fear of life and the fear of death. On the one hand the creature is

METAXY—LIFE IN-BETWEEN
A MODEL OF ADULT PSYCHOLOGY

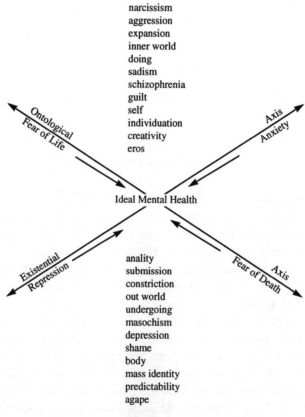

Figure 6–1

impelled by a powerful desire to identify with the cosmic process, to merge himself with the rest of nature. On the other hand he wants to be unique, to stand out as something different and apart (Becker 1973).

By "fear of life," Becker characterized that aspect of human motivation that shrinks back from fully developed individuation. The initial experience of all people is that of total dependency. While yet in the womb (we might imagine) the organism simply exists and grows in a maximally dependent state with no sense of need whatsoever. The developing fetus is kept warm by the mother's body and is fed by umbilical connection to the mother's digestive system. We might say that it is only during this period that the person is able to experience a psychological "free lunch." That is, the person is able to grow without cost, to develop without adding to the store of organismic anxiety.

Becker was not saying that the person remembers this time in any concrete sense, either consciously or unconsciously. Although he did not express himself directly on this issue, I cannot imagine that he would have met the claims of some people to have concrete prenatal memories with anything but extreme skepticism. Becker felt that one of the reasons Otto Rank's work on birth trauma was so misunderstood stemmed from the fact that he was taken too literally as inferring concrete memories of birth. Becker interpreted birth trauma as the trauma involved in leaving the known and comfortable and entering into the new and unknown.

Memories progress from interactions with objects. Even if we grant the extremely doubtful proposition that the fetal brain in the final weeks of gestation is developed enough to form and hold cognitive memories, there are simply no objects in the prenatal state to stimulate such memories. The sense of self is linguistically formed and it is difficult to see how any distinct and personal memories could be fashioned in the absence of some developed use of the linguistic first person.

However, one need not be naively credulous concerning claims to cognitive prenatal memories to posit the prenatal state as a symbol or metaphor for the desire to develop without anxiety. When psychoanalysis speaks of a desire to return to the womb, it is using the metaphor in exactly this sense—a desire to have one's needs met in an absolutely passive manner.

As the fetus is born into the world, it gets its first taste of the costs of development. It may get a cold slap on the rear or it may be eased into a tub of controlled temperature water. But regardless of the particular birthing technique, as its lungs first fill with air its status as an organism changes completely and further organismic development must be purchased by adding to the store of psychic anxiety.

Because human beings desire both consciously and unconsciously to avoid anxiety, there is, according to Becker, an ontological urge to merge with something larger than the individual. In infancy this is experienced as a desire to merge with the caregivers, to hand one's individuality over to their care and attention. As the person develops, this fear of life, this fear of individuality, may take the form of a desire to merge and be swallowed up by the family, the tribe, the nation, by oceanic nature, or even by God. The point is that there is an ontological pull, formed in the darkest recesses of even prenatal life, to passively depend on and merge with an oceanic power source that relieves the individual from the anxiety of personal responsibility for existence. When one merges self or ego into such a power source, there is a strong sensation of good feeling, of satisfaction, well-being, and plentitude.

For the human being, however, there is a price to be paid for this merger—the cost of one's own individuality. Merger finally means death to one's individuated existence, calling into play the other pull of ontology, a fear of death.

By "fear of death," Becker characterized that force of human ontology that seeks perpetuation of the self, further individuation and personal uniqueness, and independence and self-reliance. This urge is evident in the earliest stages of childhood, as the organism seeks to interact and grow by exploration and manipulation of the object world. The developing ego is propelled by its own ontological dynamics toward growth. The very sources of power merger, represented by the caregivers, can be experienced as a positive threat to this development, since merger demands development on the terms of the power source rather than on the terms of the developing ego.

Once again, however, this dynamic of ego development has its costs. For independence risks aloneness, isolation, loneliness. The world of objects is not a unilateral field for ego development. It is also an overwhelming source of danger to the isolated and lone self. Isolation stirs the anxiety of object loss, of annihilation. If the ego sticks out too far in nature, it is vulnerable to being lopped off. This sense of extreme vulnerability in the face of overwhelming power underlies all further development of individuality.

At the merger end of the ontological axis, the side of fear of life, the person enjoys the good feeling of passive safety. But it is purchased by the sacrifice of individuality. The dangers of the world are real dangers, but the ego seeks interaction in the object world. One moves out of the fear of life by repression of the real dangers in the object world. At the other end of the ontological axis, the fear of death, the ego pushes itself into the object world. It gains there the good feeling of development and accomplishment that comes from masterful manipulation of the object world. But the cost of this sense of mastery is the underlying sense of anxiety in standing isolated and alone before the real dangers of the object world. This anxiety of isolation and annihilation pushes the person back toward merger with a protective power source that is larger than the individual ego.

As Becker's ontology developed, therefore, what we see is a picture of individual motivation running between the poles of fear of life and fear of death—the pulls of merger and individuation. At the one end of this axis, the person is spurred toward the middle by repression of the fear of being swallowed up. At the other end, the person is spurred toward the middle by repression of the anxiety of isolation. A balanced middle point exists only as an ideal. Actual human life is more like a seesaw between these poles.

We might illustrate this by picturing a young child accompanied by its primary caregiver entering into a new environment—say, a petting zoo or playground. As the child enters the strange environment, it clings closely, both physically and mentally, to it caregiver, its external source of protective power. Then, as its eyes and ears begin to survey the new environment, it spots an object that demands further exploration—a puppy or another child. The child's ego projects itself into further development by interaction with this object and calls into service the dynamic of repression to quell the child's fears of the object world, allowing the child to move toward interaction with the object. Slowly but surely, the child leaves the close physical and mental protective space of the caregiver as it becomes absorbed in interaction with the object. As the child manipulates the object, the developing ego delights in its sense of growth and mastery. The child "forgets" its caregiver and indulges fully in creative mastery play with the object.

Then something unexpected happens that calls the whole process into question. The puppy barks loudly or the new playmate hits or bites. Suddenly the good feeling of manipulation and mastery grinds to a halt. The child's self feels itself too far extended, standing alone and isolated in the face of the real dangers of the object world. Overwhelmed by anxiety, the child goes running back to its caregiver, its protective power source, for assurance that it does not risk annihilation for its venture into the object world.

Then after a good cry and a few minutes of hugging comfort, the child spots a new object . . .

This illustration is sort of an idyllic picture of running along the ontological poles of human existence. Real, lived experience is rarely so clean. The child might be subject to an overly protective parent who adds to the store of anxiety of the object world and thus hinders the child from natural exploration. Likewise, a parent might be too quick to shove the child into confrontation with the object world before the child is spurred by natural curiosity, thus escalating for the child the anxiety of abandonment. The child may go scurrying back to the parent only to find that the parent is no longer sitting in the same place. The child might experience from the object something much more painful and threatening than a puppy's bark or a child's bite— perhaps a serious burn or a deep cut, thus heightening the child's fear of the dangers of the object world to overwhelming levels. Perhaps the caregiver itself is the source of the child's pain.

The child is not psychically crippled for life by one experience of merger/individuation gone awry. But when recurring patterns of anxiety-laden behavioral interactions take place over long periods of time, the tendencies of the personality—where, when, and by what the person feels threatened—are set. As the ego develops into the symbolic realm, these patterns of symbolic threats are projected in various directions. Likewise, the protective power sources on which the person relies for courage in the face of threats may also be symbolically projected in various directions. The ontological axis of fear of life and fear of death takes shape in the form of an existential axis. Life as metaxy along the existential axis, the axis of anxiety and repression, is the resulting picture Becker drew of adult psychology.

THE EXISTENTIAL AXIS

Becker viewed adult psychology as metaxy, as life in-between, as dialectical forces emanating from various existential pulls, which themselves are rooted unconsciously in the projected perception of threats and sources of protection, formed by early experience, which we explored in terms of the ontological axis. The ontological axis, the fear of life and the fear of death, Becker viewed as basic to human nature and would apply in some measure to all human beings. The existential axis represents culturally specific manifestations of the ontological dynamics. We will discuss those existential elements that apply to Western culture in the late twentieth century, that is, the era of postmodern consciousness. While individual people are focused more intently on specific dialectical pulls along the existential axis, Becker viewed all people within this culture as interacting in various degrees with each of these.

It should be stressed that in presenting human existence in terms of dialectic forces, Becker was not positing these forces as absolute dualisms. But they are felt dualisms. They are experiential dualisms. In effect, Becker was saying that human life is a confluence of opposites. But we tend in our society to think of opposites as mutually exclusive. For example, we tend to think of strength and vulnerability as mutually exclusive. To be strong means to be invulnerable. The strength of a person is registered as inversely proportional to that person's areas of vulnerability. Becker would point us toward a kind of balance in life in which, for example, strength would not be set in absolute opposition to vulnerability. In fact, conscious and thoughtful choice to maintain areas of vulnerability in one's life might be seen as a demonstration of more strength than a reflexive and frantic move to remove or hide all signs of vulnerability. In other words, while our culture pushes us toward an either/or encounter with life's opposing forces, Becker would rather point us toward an intelligent and reflective balance. With this in mind, let us look at a few of the most important of these dialectical forces.

Anality and Narcissism

In classical psychoanalytic characterology, the *anal character* refers clinically to obsessive-compulsive disorder and more generally to that type of person who exhibits orderliness, parsimony, and obstinacy. Becker used the term more expansively to refer to a style of mastering the dualism of symbolic self and animal body. The animal body is part of the object world and is subject to the real and perceived dangers of the object world. People need to symbolically escape the dangers of the object world. Symbolically evading the anxiety of these real and perceived dangers takes the form of mastery of the body, that is, mastery of the object world that the body symbolically represents. Anal characteristics result from this attempt to symbolically transcend nature. As Becker (1973) wrote, "To say that someone is 'anal' means that someone is trying extra hard to protect himself against the accidents of life and danger of death, trying to use the symbols of culture as a sure means of triumph over natural mystery, trying to pass himself off as anything but an animal" (p. 32).

In desiring order and cleanliness, excessively fearing germs and filth, the anal character seeks to protect the symbolic self from falling prey to the threats of the object world. If the object world can be ordered just right, it can present no threat. Natural anality tends one toward the preference of thorough and safe embeddedness in the cultural hero system and perceives danger in that which threatens the meanings that that system imparts. Natural anality tends one toward the fear of life, of individuality, because life and individuality represent the chaos and anarchy of nature. Money might come to represent the ultimate in the orderly symbolic triumph over nature, of a thoroughly abstract mode of compartmentalizing the arbitrariness of nature (Becker 1975).

There is a healthy form of anality, for without some measure of orderliness in life experiences, life would simply be intolerable. In its extremes, however, such as in anal-sadism, the only form of encounter with life that one can muster is to destroy it. While anality represents a constricting horror of physicalness, of death and decay, the constriction is sometimes worth the price. Better to be narrowly built into a secure world with secure meanings, into routine and the dependability of mechanical objects, than to shoulder the chaos of nature.

The other end of this continuum is narcissism. Whereas the anal tendency draws one toward the secure and shared meanings, narcissism sets oneself up as the focus of meaning for all people. Becker viewed the narcissistic urge as an expression of the "will to power." Just as there is a healthy form of anality, so is there a healthy narcissism. A measure of self-love and self-confidence is necessary for a healthy human existence. The narcissistic urge is inseparable from the desire of the ego to grow and develop. It is the urge of narcissism that aids the ego in harnessing the dynamics of repression to quell the anxieties of emerging into the object world. But in its exaggerated forms, narcissism becomes destructive by discounting and devaluing the meanings of others, of the shared meanings of culture and community. The extreme narcissist puffs up his or her project of meaning to the exclusion of shared meanings with others, in effect cutting him- or herself off from grounding in the communal protective pool of meaning. Turned inward, this inversion creates a totally unresponsive attitude toward the world. Turned outward, it can create the willingness to sacrifice countless people and objects in the pursuit of private aggrandizement and gratification.

Submission and Aggression

The earliest conscious experience of the child is that of seeking to please its caregivers. Pleasing its caregivers is the coin by which the child imagines it coaxes the caregivers into giving love and attention, which are the very foundation stones for the child's feeling of self-worth and security.

We carry this desire to please those we perceive as authorities into adult life. Submissiveness to authority is, in Becker's view, the very core of the human heart. We have already seen this in Becker's understanding of an expanded view of transference dynamics. People do not simply submit to authority because they are forced to do so. They positively seek authority figures to which they can submit. Submission relieves one of the tensions and anxieties of responsible personal existence and action. Submission is a natural response to the recognition of the overwhelming transcendence of nature. To submit and then to bask in the power of that which overwhelmingly transcends the self produces the oceanic good feeling of righteousness. Healthy submission is a realistic assessment of the fact that one's own ego is transcended in the awesome mystery of nature. As Becker wrote, it takes real strength to allow oneself to be transcended (Becker 1969).

At the other end of this continuum is aggression. Aggression represents the individual urge to resist the ego annihilation of submission, to assert one's own meanings in the face of that which transcends the ego. Aggression does not simply refer to violence. In fact, the resort to violence may be viewed as the abandonment of healthy aggression. Healthy aggression, aggression in the service of the developing ego, refers rather to a determination to resist the annihilation of being transcended and to insist on the integrity of one's own meanings and interpretations. Violent aggression often takes place in a group context and takes place more out of cowardliness than out of strength. Often it is but a compensatory act for submission to the will and authority of a leader. The leader buys the group's submission by authorizing (and shouldering the guilt for) violent aggression directed toward those weaker.

All people experience the pulls of submission and aggression. The ideal of mental health points toward a centering balance of these pulls, a balance that strives for willingness to be transcended without self-abasement and groveling, a balance that maintains a basic sense of humility in the face of power without succumbing to the urge for violent aggression as compensation for this humility. It is a balance that is the goal of personal psychological growth.

Constriction and Expansion

Personality theorists of various schools look to the constrictions placed on personality during early childhood as the source of character development. Most of the time constrictions are seen as uniformly negative and therapy is aimed at releasing the person from these constrictions. Becker also viewed constrictions as negative, but not uniformly so. A healthy kind of constriction holds the personality together, so to speak, and keeps it from flying off in all directions. Without constrictions, the person would lack a solid base for encounter and action.

The whole of reality is too much for the person to take in and digest. Therefore, personality constrictions aid the person in taking in the world of experience in manageable chunks. What makes constrictions negative is not the fact that they are constrictions but rather that, for the most part, they are reflexive and subconscious. They are imposed on the individual without the person's consent. In this view, the goal of therapy would not be simply to uniformly free the person from all constrictions, for to do so would leave the person without firm moorings in the object world.

The goal of therapy would be to make the person more consciously aware of the sources of those constrictions that are producing harmful and unwanted effects in the person's life. Although Becker realized that therapy and personal growth do not consist of insight alone, he did feel that insight, having the sources of personality constrictions revealed to the person's consciousness, is essential to the healing process. This is the beginning point for the person to take some conscious control over automatic perceptions of threats and sources of protective power.

Becker viewed neurotic constriction as a result of the suppression of symbolic choices in the face of the world of actions and objects. People hold onto a narrow range of symbolic choices as a way of evading anxiety. It is a way of tucking oneself into a secure meaning world in the choice of symbolic sources of protective power. The fetishist is the extreme example of this kind of constrictive selection of a power source, a person tucked into one peculiar source of power. But all people fetishize to some degree. The broader the person's range of sources for protective power, the more able that person will be to see a wider range of action choices in response to the object world.

Ego expansion is that force that draws the person into new experiences and discoveries in the object world. It draws the person away from the secure meanings of learned roles and behaviors in recognition that the personality is always greater than the prescribed cultural role and status of society. It is that force that allows the person to encounter others as full beings and not simply as partial beings.

Healthy expansion must be grounded, however, in a firm base of shared meaning. The pull away from the familiar, toward originality and adventure, can leave the person exposed and isolated if shared meanings are not cultivated at the same time.

All people experience the pulls of constriction and expansion. The ideal of mental health points toward a centering balance of these pulls, a balance that strives for firm grounding in secure meaning without remaining so narrow that the joy of novel experience is lost, a balance that maintains a basic sense of forward movement without flying off willy-nilly any which way. It is a balance that is the goal of personal psychological growth.

Inner World and Outer World

The transaction world of each person exists both externally and internally. Becker wrote of both an "external pole" and an "internal pole" of transaction (Becker 1964b, p. 125). He thought that individual people have preferences for one or the other sphere of transaction and that this has far-reaching effects on everything from personal styles of encounter to choices of occupation. These preferences reflect individual habits of dealing with the experiential dualism of body and self.

The internal world is the world of symbols and fantasy objects, while the external world is the world of those things we bump into. We all act in both worlds. Contact with the external world shapes personal being and identity, while bringing to bear the resources of the internal world in transacting the outer world shapes the order we impose upon it. As Becker (1967) wrote,

> The whole history of human culture is a history of the interaction of both worlds: the bringing to bear of man's fantasy-world on the hard world of nature, the

> interaction of one in the other. The symbol-world,
> taken in manageable doses, pays dividends in the real
> world. [p. 55]

Imagination is the link and mediates between these two
worlds, the symbol-world and the real world.

> Imagination is the link between new sources of energy
> within the organism and a new kind of external world
> outside it. In this way, imagination circles around the
> bind of habitual thought, and liberates new energies of
> adaptation; and it also circles around the accustomed
> facets of objects and shows them in a new light. [pp.
> 172–173]

Undergoing and Doing

Becker drew repeatedly on the work of John Dewey for his
insights. This category of doing and undergoing belongs to
Dewey. *Doing* refers to positive action in the external
world, while *undergoing* refers to the accumulation, registering, and development of the experiences of action. Both
activity and passivity are necessary components in
building up a sense of personal worth and self-esteem.

Becker saw that these two types of action play an
especially important role in the socialization process. The
child has a natural urge to act, to experiment. The human
being is a "doing" animal and this is very intense during
early childhood. Yet if the child never experiences blocks
to its actions and experimentations, the experiences
cannot be registered and reflected upon. The process of
action–blockage–reflection–action is the very process of
socialization itself. If the child experiences no blockage, we
have the makings of a sociopath. On the other hand, if the

blockage is always immediate and absolute, the child is never allowed to make its own closure on the action process and learns only a style of passive support. For this reason, Becker counseled caregivers to aim for blockage of "middle intensity" (Becker 1964b, p. 103).

Masochism and Sadism

Like Jean-Paul Sartre, Becker thought sadism and masochism come very naturally to human beings and much of human interaction can be viewed as a dance of these two forces (Sartre 1956). Because it corresponds to the experience of earliest childhood, when we were totally dependent on our caregivers for life itself, the passive, masochistic style is present in all people. We positively seek sources of power for self-merger and feel ourselves transcended and unworthy in the face of such power.

The masochistic urge is that which seeks transference merger into a source of higher power. It seeks oceanic pleasure in the act of submission to that power. Becker did write about a kind of healthy and mature masochism, a conscious, reasoned, and freely chosen self-surrender to God in the recognition of the self as fully transcended (Becker 1973). But this is not the masochism of daily life, which is reflexive and unconscious. In normal masochism, as well as in masochism as a sexual perversion, the person seeks abreactionally to make its source of pain into a source of pleasure. The act of submission is an act of self-abasement, a loss of self, closely tied to the ontological fear of life.

The masochistic surrender of self is accompanied then by the sadistic affirmation of self, as can be seen in many religious rituals, including the Christian eucharist, in which ceremonies of confession and surrender finally culminate in the symbolic or physical sacrifice of a victim (Beers 1992). Both of these styles of interaction stem from an impoverished sense of self. Becker (1969) viewed both the sadist and the masochist as worshipers of force:

> The impoverished person is the one who feels that anything that can be affirmed forcefully has value. Whether he is the one who inflicts pain or the one who suffers it, by using and submitting to force he comes under the dominion of the really real, the natural and vital. The weaker we are, the more limited is our action, but necessarily the greater is the forceful commitment with which we undertake it [p. 34]

Becker did not write of a corresponding healthy or mature sadism. He viewed the sadistic urge as that which seeks to deny the inner mystery of other people. Threatened by the intuitive sense of the inner mystery of other people, the sadist seeks to insist that only external, physical reality has any meaning. The sadist seeks to affirm his or her own mastery over death and nature by holding the fate of others in command (Becker 1975). While recognizing the fact that we all contain within us the sadistic urge, the intensity of the sadistic urge mirrors the paucity of interior resilience and strength.

Depression and Schizophrenia

Although he never expressed it quite so explicitly, Becker tended to see depression and schizophrenia as the paradigm mental disorders of the twentieth century. All people seek secure and protective sources of power for the maintenance of self-esteem. In premodern societies, the sources for such power are immediately present in the cultural *causa sui*, the cultural hero system. This usually means that the sources are very diverse, diffuse, broadly based, reflexive, and automatic.

In contemporary society, the sources of secure and protective power are constantly challenged. The result is that while a cultural *causa sui* and hero system exist, the reflexive and automatic choices are considerably narrowed for most people. The reaction of many to this is to firmly embed one's sense of self-esteem and self-worth into a rather slender sphere of one's life. It may be a career, a spouse, a child, but in any case very concentrated and limited. Placing one's sense of meaning and self-worth into such a small basket leaves one very vulnerable to having that sense of meaning and self-worth undermined by events. The loss of a job, a spouse, a child can literally mean the loss of self, of all sense of meaning and forward movement. When the blockage is total, depression is the result. From infancy, the state of total dependence is the root survival tactic of human beings. The dependent state of the depressed person reflects regression in the face of a collapse of the ability to cope, the inability to either flee or fight.

Depression is also a result of brain chemistry and the depressed person can be greatly aided by psychoactive drugs. But in viewing the phenomenon of depression in a social context of the loss of self-esteem, Becker sided with those who feel that "cognition plays a larger role in its dynamics than does physiology" (Becker 1962b, p. 26). Becker went so far as to view the self-accusing mea culpa confessions so common in sufferers of clinical depression as the fragile attempts of the person to maintain at least some sense of order in the face of a total collapse of the person's meaning world. Better to at least be able to accuse oneself of being vile and contemptible, at fault for the

workings of events, than to live in a world where such
moral categories themselves have no meaning. In this
sense, the biblical Job, who resists such interpretations of
his own misfortunes, has become the patron saint of our
time.

Becker held a long fascination, perhaps even a morbid
fascination, with the phenomenon of schizophrenia. He
wrote about schizophrenia more than any other mental
disorder, reflecting the early influence of Thomas Szasz,
who, in his attacks on involuntary incarceration based on
mental diagnosis, had made of schizophrenia the "sacred
symbol" of medicalized psychiatry. Becker's writings on
the subject tend toward a behavioral definition of the
problem, seeing it as fundamentally rooted in the self/body
dualism in which the schizophrenic literally has lost the
connection between these two aspects of human experience.

In Becker's view, the schizophrenic has grasped a
basic notion of human-meaning games that are created by
language. However, language itself is rooted in deeply felt
body meaning, which is the shared funded store of
meaning for interpersonal transactions. The schizophrenic
is one who has never been able to feel settled enough in the
body to partake of this store of shared and funded meaning. The person is left in the situation of trying to transact
with others on a purely verbal level. But since those
attempts at verbal transaction are divorced from the
shared body meanings of others, the verbal gestures
simply do not make sense in a social context. The word
symbols that the schizophrenic employs seem to float in
midair with no firm grounding in the shared experience of
others. The gestures to create transactional meaning are
genuine, but fail because the language game the person is
employing is totally personal and internal.

Becker was fascinated by the phenomenon of schizophrenia because he saw in this total divorcement of the symbol world from the body world a sort of evolutionary irony—the creation of "ultra humanity" (Becker 1964b, p. 54). If evolution had produced an animal to whom the animal body itself had become a problem, schizophrenia represented that dualism run amok.

> Schizophrenia takes the risk of evolution to its furthest point in man: the risk of creating an animal who perceives himself, reflects on himself and comes to understand that his animal body is a menace to himself . . . Man alone achieves this terrifying condition which we see in all its purity at the extremes of schizophrenic psychosis. [Becker 1973, p. 219]

These ironic musings of Becker do not detract from the fact that he held real sympathy for the sufferer of schizophrenic vulnerabilities. Rich body meanings, earned during the period of infant dependency, are the source of human repression of the fear of death. Rich body meanings are what we fall back on in the face of the terror of the object world. The schizophrenic, because he or she is not securely rooted in body meanings, has a very meager ability to repress this terror. This is a person without character defenses, so to speak, a person "for whom life is a more insurmountable problem than for others, for whom the burden of anxiety and fear is almost as constant as his daily breath" (Becker 1973, p. 217).

As the paradigm personality disorders of our time, depression and schizophrenia represent the extremes of the ontological fear of life and fear of death. Although these are the clinical edges of experience, the basic dynamics of each vulnerability are shared to some degree by many people in contemporary society. The depressed person suffers from too narrow and uncritical embeddedness in a secure and protective sphere of interpersonal meanings, while the schizophrenic has been cut off entirely from the sphere of shared interpersonal meanings.

Shame and Guilt

In Becker's presentation of adult psychology, the dialectic of shame and guilt refers to psychological blocks to action in the object world. Shame occurs when one has abjectly transgressed a clear and shared social taboo. To experience shame, the feeling that makes one want to simply hide, the person must share the social and cultural worldview of those around him or her. Shame is the internal emotional result of flaunting the behavioral norms that, in a particular sociocultural environment, represent the mode of merger with secure and protective sources of power. While internal, shame is a very public emotion. As a block to action, originating in the merger end of the ontological axis, shame functions as a social sanction aimed at keeping the fund of shared social meaning intact. As Becker (1964b) wrote, "In a world of confusion, change and mobility, shame sanctions would operate with difficulty, if at all. One is truly shamed before his cultural peers, rarely fully before foreigners" (p. 193).

Guilt originates at the opposite end of the ontological axis. Becker wrote of various types of guilt. In contemporary society, a most common source of guilt occurs when the norms of the society in which one presently lives differ greatly from the rules of behavior one was taught. Guilt often focuses on behaviors relating to sex, use of financial resources, and responsibilities toward the extended family, for these are areas in which the norms of late-capitalist society are most likely to differ from what one was taught in the family.

A more vague but pervasively diffuse type of guilt in modern society is that of existential guilt, which is closely related to the body/self dualism of human life. The body can be experienced as a genuine drag on the ideal freedom of the individual. This is another reason why guilt and sex form a complex unity. Sexual intercourse is the acme of giving in to creature, species, and body meanings. While these meanings form the basis of personal identity, these meanings also tend to deny one's sense of uniqueness and specialness in the world. As Becker (1973) wrote, "guilt is there because the body casts a shadow on the person's inner freedom, his 'real self' that—through the act of sex—is being forced into a standardized, mechanical, biological role" (p. 42). The controls one places on sexual behavior point toward the human need to remove the act of intercourse from being purely an animal act. Likewise, the slang often employed in speaking about persons who appear to have no controls over their sexual behavior (which are mostly animal metaphors—rabbits, dogs, pigs) point in this same direction.

Becker (1973) saw that this kind of animal guilt is increased when sex is pursued in the absence of love. The dynamic of love in the sexual relationship "allows the collapse of the individual into the animal dimension without fear and guilt, but instead with the trust and assurance that his distinctive inner freedom will not be negated by an animal surrender" (p. 42).

The guilt of the body/self dualism is, as various existential philosophers have put it, the guilt of being itself. It is the guilt of a dependent being in the face of overwhelmingly transcendent power. It is the guilt of simply taking up space, and knowing it. As Becker (1975) wrote, "It reflects the self-conscious animal's bafflement at having emerged from nature, at sticking out too much without knowing what for, at not being able to securely place himself in an eternal meaning system" (p. 158).

Body and Self

A fundamental experiential dialectic is that of body and self. Since at least the time of Plato this dialectic has been at the center of the Western philosophical tradition. Though countless attempts have been made to mediate this dialectic in one way or another, it is felt experientially by any reflective person and therefore simply will not go away. It is a perennial human issue.

Becker's presentation of the oedipal transition and the socialization process clearly demonstrates why this is so. In that transition from a body-self to a symbol-self that is the socialization process, the body must become an object to the self in order for the body to be placed firmly under the control of the self. In other words, the very earliest experience the person has of the symbolic self is that of the self objectifying the body and seeking to control the body. Making the body an object for control by the symbolic self is the very core of, for example, toilet training. The child may even drive itself to constipation in the attempt to prove how well it can "hold" the body in check. There is simply no way around the fact that the experiential dialectic of body and self is deeply embedded in the psyche of all people.

There are philosophical and psychological ontologies that radicalize this body/self dialectic beyond proper measure, and these have been rightly criticized.[1] Much of Christian ideology has fallen into this category, by so strongly valuing the soul that the body comes to be seen as unimportant or even evil. At present we seem to be going through a period of reaction to this type of theology. The current trend seems to be toward various types of body philosophies. If the spirit of Dionysus is not invoked somewhere in a book or essay, the work will surely not be well received in some important circles.

Becker's work on the body/self dialectic helps us to understand why ideologies that exalt the cognitive and debase the physical have often been adopted by the forces of oppression in this world. But his work also stands as a strong caution against seeking our salvation in an equally unbalanced move in the opposite direction. The merger and loss of self in the indulgence of body meaning has as its underside the reflexive affirmation of self in the sadistic ingestion of the body. Let us not forget in our ecstatic affirmation of the body that the Dionysian orgy culminates in ritual sacrifice and even cannibalism.

The felt dualism of body and self cannot be simply denied or ignored. Such moves are doomed to failure because they violate the foundational experiences of human personality. The balance required acknowledges and gives due to both body meaning and symbolic self meaning.

---

1. A few reviewers have placed Becker's work among those who would exalt the cognitive and intellectual and debase the body. I feel strongly that such reviewers have arrived at this conclusion by very cursory readings of Becker's works, and by taking single quotes out of context. They have fundamentally misunderstood Becker's work both as to intent and in terms of solid content.

The body is an object to the self. The self discovers its body as an instrument in possession of the self, an instrument to situate the self in the world of objects. The human self, or consciousness, comes into being by its interaction with others. Its objectification of the body as an instrument to be controlled is made largely in response to other people, to the demands of the social world. Becker (1964b) stressed this by referring to the self as "an amalgam of social motives" (p. 241), such that the self can only intellectually comprehend that it is by necessity lodged in an animal body. The self feels itself to be immortal—it can imagine itself in almost any condition, except that of not existing. (This, I think, is the reason there continues to be power behind the Cartesian dictum, *cogito, ergo sum*, even though this has been roundly rejected as an epistemic starting point.) Yet it knows, intellectually, that it is bound to a mortal body and that finally the body will have the last word.

The body, therefore, feels strange to the self, as a foreign element. We may lose a limb, an eye, an ear and still be happy that "I" am still here. When pressed, most adults would probably point to their head to locate the "real me" in the body. That is, after all, where thinking takes place. Current science fiction often assumes that so long as the brain remains the same, the audience will be satisfied that a self is retained, even if that brain is moved from body to body. Yet the ancient Egyptians, who took great pains to mummify various vital organs, sucked the brain out through the nose of the corpse and tossed it to the dogs! Many ancient traditions have located the real self in the heart, or even the bowels. Children seem to prefer the chest or stomach region for locating the "real me."

The body is a symbolic instrument of the self. And just as the self can feel itself untouched by the loss of body parts—we hardly agonize over a haircut or nail trim—the self can also extend its symbolic instrument beyond the skin of the body. Almost any object can become body to the symbolic self such that the loss of that object is experienced as traumatically as, or even more traumatically than, an injury or disfigurement of the physical body. We may laugh at a character in a television sitcom who would rather lose an arm than have a scratch on his car. But we understand the joke.

All of this simply underlines the fact that the body/self dialectic is a felt experience of human beings. It is inseparable from what we know as self-consciousness, that which separates humans from other animal species.

Body meanings and self meanings are both integral aspects of human experience. Body meanings are those that tie us to the earth, to species, to merger. Self meanings are those of uniqueness, soaring above nature, of individuation. Personal, spiritual, and psychological growth demands attention to both aspects of meaning in our lives.

A perfect balance between these aspects of our existence is rarely achieved. It is in one sense our life quest. Becker (1973) wrote, "The basic problem of life, in this sense, is whether the species (body) will predominate over one's individuality (inner self)" (p. 226).

Our basic styles of working on this problem of life have been set for each of us in the course of the oedipal transition. For some, family styles have invested the body with an extra dose of anxiety and denial, resulting perhaps in adulthood in draining and debilitating hypochondrias and phobias. For others, family styles may have so belittled the life of the mind that the adult person must cope with real blockage and guilt for fostering his or her intellect. Becker (1968b) felt that one very useful way of approaching and attempting to understand what is taking place in the so-called sexual perversions is to view it in the patient as a "problem of the aesthetic integration of spirit (personality) and body" (p. 178). The particular perversion is viewed as the symbol game the patient must play in allowing the aesthetic merger of body and self to culminate in the sexual act.

All people experience the pulls of body and symbolic self. The ideal of mental health points toward a centering balance of these pulls, a balance that strives for the fostering of body meanings without neglect of the intellect, a balance that maintains a basic sense of the spiritual life without discounting or devaluing the physical life. It is a balance that is the goal of personal psychological growth.

Mass Being and Individuality

A person may ask, "What is the meaning and purpose, the value, of my life?" Becker said this question is being posed and in some sense answered in even the most mundane and routine thoughts and actions of everyday living. It is a natural and unavoidable urge of human ontology that the person wants his or her life to count, to make a difference, to mean something. This is the basic urge toward heroism. All human beings pursue the heroic—the safe heroics of the crowd or the dangerous heroics of individuation.

The heroics of the crowd keep one well protected within the sphere of shared meaning. The mass being can answer personally for his or her actions, we might say, by pointing to others who are doing the same thing. In effect, we have here the child's alibi, "They did it first! Don't ask me, ask them!" The culture and society offer opportunities for heroism enough for the mass being. To be referred to on occasion as the bread winner, or a civic-minded person, is satisfying enough of the urge toward uniqueness. The mass being accepts the very standardized transference authorities of the culture—parents, the boss at work, the parish minister, and so on—and tucks in warmly to their symbolic powers of security and protection, seeking only to please them. The heroism of the mass being is a species or collective heroism—as progenitor or group member. The urge to heroism is answered by that which is safest, given, nearest to hand.

True individual heroism is not so easily achieved and is even harder to sustain. Individual heroism strives for that which is unique, that which stands out from the crowd. The heroic individual wants to earn for him- or herself the recognition that the mass being is willing to have simply as one member of the group. The heroic individual seeks adventure and novelty, considering safety and routine tantamount to death.

Human beings are seekers of meaning and purpose and need both to live. The earliest sense of meaning and purpose was gained passively, almost by osmosis, from our primary caregivers. Even through adolescence and young adulthood, the sense of meaning and purpose we have comes primarily from doing what other people tell us to do. It is little wonder, then, that so many people easily accept the safety and security of cultural and species heroics. There is nothing to disparage about this, other than the fact that it causes to go to waste untold amounts of creative human potential.

Individual heroics, on the other hand, leaves one open and vulnerable to the onrush of anxiety. The heroic individual, in attempting to transcend the standardized heroics of the crowd, must create his or her own meaning and then offer that up as its own justification. This is not an easy task for anyone because our very character and personality system has been formed as a defense against anxiety. To stand alone with one's own sense of meaning and purpose is anxiety provoking. In a very real sense, the act of standing alone with the meaning and purpose one has created as a heroic individual risks directly undermining one's personality and character. It is little wonder that the leader keeps looking back to make sure others are following!

If the holistic personality is to flourish, there must be rooting in shared meanings, the cultural and species heroics of the community. On the other hand, one firmly rooted in the shared meanings, the cultural and species heroics of the community, must also be encouraged to cultivate areas of uniqueness and individuality. Becker (1973) suggested that what is needed is the creation of "maximum individuality within maximum community" (p. 251). He recognized this as a paradox, not one that can be achieved by public policy, even in a democracy. But as an ideal-typical balance of the polarity of mass being and individual, it is a goal toward which to labor.

Predictability and Creativity

The polarity of predictability and creativity focuses on issues of aesthetics. In Becker's view, aesthetics is a process of interaction between the established and shared meanings of the culture and society and the innovative and novel meanings of the individual.

There are aesthetic creations that are so embedded in the established and shared meanings of the culture and society that their effect is simply to confirm and further establish those meanings. There is no challenge in such creations, but only a soothing acceptance of the standardized, conventional, and traditional transference objects that the majority of people already share. One thinks here of elevator Muzak, which assures the person ascending or descending the floors of a large office building that, yes, here is power, here is protection, here is a quiet and solemn fortress of strength that you can serve and in which you can perform your tasks of buying, banking, and business in calm serenity. One thinks of the commercial arts, which confirm people in their role as consumers of goods, sanctioning them in the process of extending their sense of personal worth into the accumulation of the newest, the fastest, the best trinkets that the economic system has to offer. One thinks of the sweet paintings of Christ, gathering his cherubic children around him, placidly reflecting back to faces of admiration and gratitude the secure and safe promise of their worthiness before God.

On the other hand, there are aesthetic creations that are nothing but offensive, that assault the audience with total rejection of all the values, sense of worth, and objects of esteem they commonly share. One thinks here of the worst kinds of rock and roll music, of performance artists who smear themselves with excrement, or of the creations in various media that consciously seek the sacrilege. Challenging, perhaps, but the audience shrinks back almost in terror. The audience wants to scream out, "But is this art?!"

Predictability is an essential element of meaning in human existence. Culture and society have developed complex systems of predictability, from role and status, which allow a person to have some idea of what to expect in transactions with people, to electronic tracking devices, which provide travelers with weather information regarding their flights. Where there is no sense of predictability, where there is no sense of regularity and order, there is no sense of meaning. Without at least some sense of meaning and predictability, of perceivable cause-and-effect sequences, the person is left exposed and vulnerable, open to almost any suggestion that holds the promise of restoring order and regularity. This is a fact of human existence that is not lost on the various demonic brain-washers, from wardens of political prison camps to leaders of religious cults.

Yet a steady diet of easy aesthetic mergers, which do nothing but confirm and support the shared meanings of social and cultural heroics, can only lead to stagnation of the human spirit. People seek mergers of assurance, protection, and safety. But they also seek to be challenged, to dig deeper, to have their folly exposed to them. The ideal aesthetics, in this view, would be those creations that both assure and challenge. It would be those creations that build on the familiar and predictable, but allow the audience to see these matters in a new way. It would be those creations that draw the audience in through standardized social and cultural heroics, but do not ignore or deny the underside, the shadow side of that reality. It would be those creations that present the audience with this shadow side of reality, but point toward salvation at the same time. As Becker (1973) wrote,

> The creative person becomes then, in art, literature and religion, the mediator of natural terror and the indicator of a new way of triumph over it. He reveals the darkness and the dread of the human condition and fabricates a new symbolic transcendence over it.
> [p. 220]

Becker, expanding here on the insights of Rank (1968), saw clearly that the problem of aesthetics, the problem of what is "true" art and what is simply everyday aesthetics, is a direct reflection of the problem of human ontological polarity itself.

> The aesthetic object demonstrates that life is not in vain, by holding up tangible proof of human creativity. Thus we see the difference between the true artist and the everyday aesthetician: the everyday aesthetician secures conviction by nestling the human spirit in its familiar cultural bonds. The true artist . . . overcomes the arbitrary cultural fiction by allowing man to believe in his basic creativity. [Becker 1964b, p. 239]

This places a very heavy burden on the true artist. The true artist is one who has seen through the fictional character of the shared system of cultural heroics. Having seen through this veneer, the artist is no longer able to draw his or her personal sense of meaning from that secure and protective source of power—or at least only tentatively and falteringly. The artist must, instead, fashion novel and very personal sources of meaning and conviction and then offer them up to the audience in the hope that these meanings will be confirmed by the community of fellows. In other words, the true artist lives in a state of being that is constantly threatened by loneliness and isolation. This is why, as Becker saw, the truly great artists in human history have often lived their lives very far toward the schizophrenic end of the human continuum. The confirmation of the worth and value of the artist's work is often postponed until long after the artist is dead—until society has caught up to the artist's aesthetic vision. How many of our greatest artists have died in poverty, loneliness, and rejection! The artist is doomed to an existence that is often almost indistinguishable from mental illness. Diagnosing great artists of the past has become almost a cottage industry in the world of psychiatric literature. To put it somewhat provocatively, the main difference between a true artist and a prosaic manic or schizophrenic boils down to the very intangible element of talent.

While therapeutic biases lean toward seeking balance between the predictable and the creative, it must be recognized at the same time that had Da Vinci, Mozart, Van Gogh, Kierkegaard, Nietzsche, not to mention Jimi Hendrix or Janis Joplin, been therapized and attained more balance, our world would be much poorer for it. Who could possibly say that we would be willing to live without the great aesthetic works they produced? Yet who could be so cruel as to wish the lives of these people on any fellow human being? This is not even to mention the lives of their families and close acquaintances, for while we appreciate the artistic productions of such people, let's face it squarely, the artistic muse is one of extreme narcissism, and many such people pollute their environment with their poisoned personalities. Is the creative and challenging aesthetic vision that these people have given to humanity worth the immense pain and personal anguish that had to be suffered in order to produce it? No one can answer that question without resort to religious metaphysics. Reflecting on this problem, Becker (1968b) wrote "the radical innovator may be the very instrument of creative evolution itself" (p. 232).

Agape and Eros

We finally come in this exploration of various cultural expressions of the ontological polarity of human existence to those ancient distinctions of love, agape love, and eros love. It is the distinction between the love that is expressed as self-surrender and the love that is expressed as self-expression. It is a category of polarity that brings to philosophical closure each of the polarities we have been discussing.

The agapic love expressed in self-surrender! To take the

existential burden of living and place it at the feet of that overwhelming power that transcends the self! What a blissful and oceanic relaxation this brings!

The erotic love expressed in self-expression! To assert one's own personal strength and value in the face of that overwhelming power that transcends the self and deflates the ultimate meaning of subjectivity! What a sense of intense vitality and energy this brings!

These pulls toward Agape and Eros summarize Becker's model of a mature adult psychology. Because perfect and sustainable balance can only be offered as an ideal-typical vision, it is finally a model of tragedy, a model of a very peculiar species that is torn by the forces of its very being.

> Now we see what we might call the ontological or creature tragedy that is so peculiar to man: If he gives in to Agape he risks failing to develop himself, his active contribution to the rest of life. If he expands Eros too much he risks cutting himself off from the healing power of gratitude and humility that he must naturally feel for having been created, for having been given the opportunity of life experience . . . You can see that man wants the impossible: He wants to lose his isolation and keep it at the same time . . . He wants to expand by merging with the powerful beyond that transcends him, yet he wants while merging with it to remain individual and aloof, working out his own private and smaller-scale self-expansion. [Becker 1973, p. 155]

Becker saw that the only really satisfying answer to the human dilemma would be a Creator God, a God who is the origin of human individuation itself, the very author of natural and human creativity. Only such a God could accept and give final meaning and purpose to the creative gifts offered up by a gracious and humble individual without simultaneously so overwhelming that individual with transcendent power that merger in surrender would demand the relinquishment of the achievements of individuation itself.

Thus Becker finally found in the ontological restlessness of the human experience, which he discovered through the methods of empirical social science, a point that the Psalmist knew from ancient times: "As a doe longs for running streams, so longs my soul for you, My God. My soul thirsts for God, the God of life" (Psalm 42:1–2).

Of course, that is hardly an easy prescription to the human dilemma. For every god that we encounter in everyday life is a god mediated through the institutional structures of the culture and society. In short, the only gods we have available for immediate and mass consumption are exactly those gods that are standardized and conventional transference objects, projections of the social status quo. The god toward which Becker pointed is itself an ideal-typical construct for which there is no overwhelming evidence even of its concrete existence. Seeking such a god is on a practical level indistinguishable from seeking those ideal-typical balances of existential and ontological polarity. There is nothing that privileges the religious avenue for this quest above the avenue of the psychological or other secular course. The choice of one's path, whether the quest shall be religious or secular, finally comes down to the individual's arbitrary and pluralistic preferences that have been formed in the process of early character development.

So where has Becker finally left us? Are we any better off than before this journey of exploration? If our hope was for self-assured mergers, easily attained aesthetic closures, and "gain without pain" in our quest for spiritual, mental, and personal growth, we can only be disappointed. We find in Becker no quick fixes, no therapeutic tricks or techniques, that will dissolve Gethsemane, that will allow us to avoid the dark night of the soul. It can only be encountered, now giving deepest spiritual and psychological meaning to the Christian formula "by Grace, through Faith" (Forde 1982).

Yet for those who are determined, who feel compelled toward truth regardless of the costs, Becker's work does offer the bittersweet solace that the quest for an ideal-typical transference object is not there on a take-it-or-leave-it basis. It is at the very heart and core of human existence itself.

Therapy Beyond Becker

*We don't expect happiness
from each other, just each other.*

S. J. Marks

THE LIMITS OF THERAPY, *NOCH EINMAL*

What makes people act the way they do? Becker has given us a penetrating analysis and exposition of the tragedy of human existence. Psychological and pastoral counseling seeks to bring healing and growth to those who request it. Becker seems to have left us in a position that finally, with Miguel de Unamuno, stresses the "tragic sense of life," with the sad warning that there is no uncomplicated and effortless healing. There is only further stumbling along the road of life. To where? Maybe nowhere.

There is no question that as Becker delved deeper and deeper into the human psyche, he lost his earlier optimism about the human predicament. If there is a clear-cut distinction to be made between the early Becker and the mature Becker (bearing in mind that we are speaking here of a time span of less than 15 years!), it is exactly at that point of optimism concerning human possibilities. Steeped in the tradition of Enlightenment humanism, the early Becker spoke of a Second Great Step in human evolution, of the liberating possibilities of insight and self-knowledge, of emancipation of the human spirit through education, and steady but illuminated tinkering with social structures. By the time we come to the mature Becker, he had come to see the human being in quite a different light—far from courageous and heroic, but terrified, guilt-ridden, and cowering creatures, more than ready to offer up anyone but themselves to keep their defenses intact. He saw that the shadow side of the human character, the masochistic/sadistic polarity, was much more deeply rooted than an optimistic humanism could possibly admit or imagine. Even that urge for more life, that ontological urge toward individuation that is the very source of all the Enlightenment tradition pictured as admirable and laudable in the human species, was fatefully tainted by the base craving to stand smiling over the corpses of those whom one has slaughtered! With pain that has not been lost on this reader, the dying Becker wrote,

> The reason is positive and simple: man aggresses not only out of frustration and fear but out of joy, plenitude, love of life. *Men kill lavishly out of the sublime joy of heroic triumph over evil. Voilà tout.* What are the clinical classifications and niceties going to do with that? [Becker 1975, p. 141, emphasis original]

It is enough to make one who would desire to bring healing and growth to human life want to close the corpus of Becker's work with a chilling shudder, to repress its very message and quietly hope that he could not have meant these words!

If this is a true picture of the human being, it totally demolishes the utopianism of psychotherapy. The utopian assumption underlying psychotherapy is that by liberating people from the constricting influences of past socialization life can become free and unconstricted. Becker's work insists that the real sources of constriction are internally imposed at least as much as externally imposed. This being the case, psychotherapy can, at best, help to relieve specific, identified symptoms. The person is left with his or her basic personality and character armor unchanged and may well find that the specific symptoms have simply shifted, not disappeared (which may or may not be perceived by that person as a therapy success). Becker's work forces us to the conclusion that neurosis is normal—that is, that normalcy is neurotic. Furthermore,

> once you accept the truly desperate situation that man is in, you come to see not only that neurosis is normal, but that even psychotic failure represents only a little additional push in the routine stumbling along life's way. [Becker 1973, p. 269]

If the utopianism of psychotherapy in terms of the individual cannot stand up to critical scrutiny, how much less is its currency as a foundation for social policy. The psychotherapist or counselor who confronts the work of Becker will be quite sobered concerning the prospects of this enterprise. The overall Beckerian perspective is pessimistic. Like the sobering views of Reinhold Niebuhr, Becker's pessimism can be interpreted as supportive of neoconservative political policy. It undermines the utopian radicalism of the Left. But Becker's pessimism is not that of the political conservative, who simply wants a continuation of the status quo. He is even more critical of present

political structures, the very source of continued alienation, than he is of the utopian Left. It is an intelligent and
thoughtful pessimism that I have found impossible to
ignore. I feel that in spite of its overall pessimism, there is
much to be gained from fully confronting Becker's work,
sobering though it may be.

Another issue in which the psychotherapist may benefit from fully digesting Becker's thought is increased
depth in the understanding of countertransference. The
psychotherapist or counselor has a duty to uphold the
highest standards of professional ethics and professional
demeanor. Essential to the therapeutic enterprise is the
setting and maintaining of professional "distance" in the
therapeutic relationship. This is a given.

However, one aspect of the shadow side of this maintenance of professional distance is the subtle placement of
judgments of value on the therapist/client relationship.
Because of the inequality in the power relationship between therapist and client, it is very difficult for the
therapist to avoid placing him- or herself above the client,
to avoid a mental opposition between the "sick" and the
"healthy," to avoid a subtle air of superiority.

Consider the act of "diagnosis"—literally, "through-
knowing." In effect, the therapist is saying, "I know you
through and through. You don't know me, but I know you.
I will tell you what your problem is." It is necessary to the
therapeutic enterprise, but it is hardly an act of mutuality.
Yet the therapist, if he or she is at all authentically in touch
with the dynamics of human psychological reality, must
be carrying at least as much pain as the client. The
therapist also has had to constrict and repress his or her
ego expansion in the course of becoming adult. If the
therapist is not in touch with his or her own pain, it
becomes very likely that this pain (perhaps in the guise of

therapeutic distance) will be projected onto the patient. If the goal of therapy is healing, it must happen in the context of dyadic woundedness and pain. Henri Nouwen's image of the "wounded healer" here comes to mind as an empirical description of the therapeutic relationship.

The problem of countertransference is made more acute by the fact that psychology is very much itself a system of fictitious heroics through which those who have committed themselves to its practice earn their sense of self-esteem and worth. It contains its own doctrines, its secret "gnosis," reserved for the initiated. It tends to create in groups and out groups, with all of the dynamics involved in that process, between those who serenely "know" and those who remain in ignorance. Psychotherapists and counselors share to one degree or another in that fictitious system of heroics. The client has entered into their territory, their turf, seeking their expertise. This only increases the difficulty of keeping the fictitious nature of the psychotherapeutic hero system well in mind in relating to the client.

Even Freud, who certainly understood the dynamics of transference and countertransference, was not immune to the feelings of superiority toward which psychotherapy tends. In response to Freud's assessment of human beings on the whole, "In my experience most of them are trash . . ." Becker (1973) wryly commented,

> Of course, he also implies that if most people are trash, some aren't, and we can surmise who is one of the few exceptions. We are reminded of those once-popular books on eugenics that always carried a handsome frontispiece photograph of the author beaming his vitality and personality as the ideal type of the book's argument. [p. 256]

Becker reminded us that our most basic problems always extend beyond the reach of psychotherapy. While it is true that the person who presents for therapy is seeking in the therapist the merger with a safe and secure transference object, the therapist is a person as well. The therapist must earn his or her own sense of self-value within a fictitious system of heroics. Therapists have their own sources of ambivalence and dependency. Therapists have their own objects of transference before which they cower in humble gratitude. If the therapist shoulders the burden of the client's need for a transference object, the difference between therapist and client remains one of degree, not of kind. "In the game of life and death no one stands taller than any other" (Becker 1973, p. 259).

If Becker is pessimistic about the utopianism of therapy and counseling, it must be understood that he was writing in reaction to some of the more wild claims for therapy, counseling, and experiential encounter groups that were current on the West Coast during the late 1960s and early 1970s. Humanistic-oriented psychology had at that time reached a sort of acme of optimism, both in terms of experimental methods and in terms of the exaggerated professions of healing, incite, and liberation. To this environment, Becker brought the sober reminders of an empirical scientific mind. If being human is the final problem of Human Being, contended Becker, if Death is the final and absolute annihilation of the human organism, representing the irrevocable defeat of the whole process of individuation and psychological growth, then psychology is severely limited in the extent to which it can give answers to the human problem. To pretend otherwise could lead, at best, away from psychology and into religion. If that is the move that therapy in search of utopia takes, then Becker demanded that they at least be honest about it.

These therapies represent a flight of the human spirit and need not be totally disparaged. On the other hand, as Becker saw so clearly, when the spirit is cultivated in a manner that ignores the body meanings of human Being, that is, when one side of human ontology is pursued in neglect or denial of the other polarity, it cannot produce enduring results. The insistence of "mind over matter" is ephemeral at best, and can leave one dangerously vulnerable to unconscious, reflexive, and regressive backlash. During the past twenty years we have watched these therapies reap the harvest of the seeds sown.

These therapies have moved in several directions, some more honest than others. The most honest direction has been to considerably scale back claims for results, as participants have continued to experience depression, neurosis, and even psychosis, often resulting directly from the lifestyles and substances that were once touted as the key to liberation. These therapies, in chastened form, continue to be useful for some people.

Another direction that also has some claim for honesty has been that of frankly admitting that the therapy has moved out of psychology and into religion with the overt adoption of religious myth and metaphysics as a supporting leg. Such new religions can offer adherents on a smaller scale what established religions have offered the masses of humanity throughout history. This can be valuable for those whose disenchantment with established religion has been so complete that they simply can no longer identify with the historical religions. For those whose disenchantment is not so total, this move into religious sectarianism may not seem very attractive. Such people will perhaps be drawn back into the historical stream of the established religions, albeit with new interpretations and understandings reflecting various sectarian influences.

Less-honest directions we have seen from this mush-rooming of therapies (Kyle 1993) have included both the devolution into overt cults based on adoration of a leader (est, Scientology, Synanon) and the cultivation of spirituality while at the same time encouraging a most crassly individualistic, acquisitive, and consumeristic appease-ment of the flesh (Silva Mind Control, various Zen sects, and some New Age groups).

Honest psychological and pastoral counseling will draw back from the utopianism of both pop therapies and the metaphysics of new religions. A thorough encounter with the work of Becker will be a great aid in discerning reality from utopianism. However, I do not feel that this thorough encounter leaves the therapist or counselor par-alyzed in the face of the real human desire for personal and psychological growth. In seeking a therapy beyond Becker, I would like to point to just a few avenues open to the honest psychological or pastoral counselor, which I will designate as intimations of transcendence. It should be clear that I am not here speaking of the transcendence of death but rather the transcendence of debilitating death anxiety. It should also be clear in what follows that in my attempts to point toward a therapy beyond Becker, I am not disputing any particular position of Becker, nor Beck-er's specific words. Rather I am suggesting that it is his philosophical approach in general that stands in need of reflective supplementation.

INTIMATIONS OF TRANSCENDENCE

Unity of Body and Spirit

Becker was a true inheritor of the Western philosophical tradition, which places body and spirit, or body and soul, in opposition. As we saw, this dualism is supported by solid empirical evidence of the socialization process. The body indeed becomes an object in the field of the self. It cannot be simply ignored or denied and Becker was rightly suspicious of those approaches that are based on the denial of this fundamental dualism. However, even Becker insisted that this dualism is a perceived dualism, an heuristic dualism, and not an absolute or metaphysical dualism. This leaves the window open, as a goal of therapy and personal growth (not as a beginning point!) for the reconciliation or uniting of body meaning with spiritual meaning.

The psychological and pastoral counselor may want to introduce into therapy perspectives that hold this goal of unity, as that toward which to strive, more explicitly than does Becker. Such perspectives will be countercultural in a cultural atmosphere in which the standardized heroics tend to further this separation rather than to aim toward reconciliation. I personally have found very helpful on this point the metaphors of anima/animus gleaned from archetypal psychology (Hillman 1985, Hopcke 1989).

In our society, males are socialized to prize the intellect above all else, including the secure body meanings of the physical world. A traditionally male spirituality naturally tends in this same direction, of radicalizing the opposition of intellect and body rather than facilitating closer reconciliation. Becker recognized this as a problem in need of solution. But Becker (1974a) also admitted that, if for no other reason than that it better suited his temperament, his spirituality was Apollonian as opposed to Dionysian. Perhaps because females have traditionally been socialized to prize their childbearing ability, while experiencing the pride of intellect through the accomplishments of their husbands, it seems to be easier for women to integrate body meanings into their spirituality. One hopes this is not lost as women, pursuing justice and equality, seek to be more like men.

Keeping well in mind, therefore, that masculine and feminine are fundamentally social constructions, I have found that recognition and cultivation of the feminine within myself have had the joyous side effect of tempering one-sided masculine spirituality with feminine body-meanings. I lay no claim to significant personal accomplishment in this movement toward unity. But for me personally, this has been very useful in my attempts to overcome the worst prejudices and constrictions of the masculine socialization I have experienced in this culture. While I maintain a strong skepticism of archetypal psychology as a system (particularly those forms that seem to grant the various archetypes a reified and independent existence outside of the individual), I have experienced this process of touching the feminine within myself as a clear intimation of transcendence.

Death as a Source of Enhanced Reflection

Becker saw death, the final and absolute annihilation of the human organism, as the ultimate limitation, as that which gives lie to all of human striving and heroism. Because death cannot be overcome, we must conclude with Qoheleth, that "All is vanity! For all his toil, his toil under the sun, what does man gain by it?" (Ecclesiastes 1:1–3).

Well, yes, it is very difficult to move beyond that bit of biblical wisdom. Death creates a panic in the human breast that is not easily calmed except by layer upon layer of repression. On the other hand, there are those who testify to the possibility of living with death as an ally in life, an ally that helps them to cut through the vanities of standardized cultural heroism, to recognize and concentrate on what is really important.

Much of the reaction to the testimonies of those who have been through near-death experiences, associated with the work and research of Elisabeth Kübler-Ross (1969) and Raymond A. Moody, Jr. (1975, 1977), has been at the rather superficial level of seeking easy merger with death in the assurance of an afterlife. However, I have been more impressed with the testimonies of such people to the real changes in living that their death encounters have produced. Many of these people have genuinely made death awareness an ally in life. This has produced for them changes in values, in what they see as important, and in how they allocate their time and resources.

Again, I lay no claim to personal achievement in this area. I go through periods when the existential angst of the reality of death, of personal annihilation, is all but overwhelming. Yet I see in the testimonies of these people and others like them a clear intimation of transcendence, an intimation that points toward the possibility of incorporating the immediate awareness of death (which is not the same as awareness of immediate death!) as an ally in life, an ally that enhances concentration on what is important, allowing one to let go of failures and injustices that constrict and deform life away from those values that are most important. This incorporation of death awareness as an ally in life, the consciousness of finitude and limits, is one very potent way of getting at that style of living that many religious traditions have pointed toward in the metaphor of new birth, of dying that one might live. We may add the weight of these traditions to the testimonies of others in encountering this as a clear intimation of transcendence, as a goal of therapy and personal growth.

Irving Yalom (1980) wrote in a similar vein of the benefits of incorporating death awareness into the process of therapy. While remaining aware that death is a primary source of anxiety that cannot be minimized, he wrote, "The incorporation of death into life enriches life; it enables individuals to extricate themselves from smothering trivialities, to live more purposefully and more authentically" (p. 54). Much of what Becker wrote on death denial and death anxiety would lead one to the conclusion that this incorporation of death awareness as an ally in life is more or less impossible. Yet Becker himself came to a similar understanding as he faced his own death (Becker 1974a).

The Paradigm of Relationship

Becker followed closely the object relations school of psychoanalysis in his formulations of human motivation and human interactions. This is defensible both in terms of what is current in the field as well as by the fact that the phenomenological and existential models of philosophy, which were so influential on Becker's mature thought, tend one toward viewing the world from the radically subjective perspective. As a mode of perceiving and presenting the problem of human living, this is a very useful tool of analysis.

Without disputing the benefits of this approach, one must finally ask whether this is the only way of perceiving human motivation and human interaction. What are the alternatives, and what are the strengths and weaknesses of object relations theory when compared with alternative approaches?

I have found the object relations approach to be useful in outlining the kinds of cognitive and emotional processes that take place in the course of human development, especially in the earliest stages. But in terms of trying to comprehend a more mature adult psychology, I have found important blind spots in the radicalized subject/object frame of reference that the object relations perspective assumes. These blind spots are found equally in the approaches of existential philosophy as represented by Heidegger, Kierkegaard, and Sartre as well.

To focus directly on the most important of these blind spots, this approach leaves very little space for genuine and mutual relationship between people, which is squeezed too tightly into the extreme subject/object mode. This forces the subject into an objectification of those with whom relationship is sought. Objectification is, almost by definition, destructive of genuine and mutual relationship. In other words, the very frame of reference for analysis precludes a priori the possibility of achieving the genuine and mutual relationship that one seeks. This would not be a problem if, in fact, genuine and mutual relationships do not exist. But a very large number of people do indeed feel that they have had the experience of relationships that are genuine and mutual. An approach to analysis that negates a priori such a large and meaningful chunk of human experience without solid and demonstrative evidence for the negation—saying, in effect, "This is not what you say it is," even though people consistently report that it feels that way to them—must be supplemented by alternative points of view that allow the experience of people to be treated more seriously and sympathetically.

Becker shied away from soft interpretations of human relationships such as I am proposing here as a supplement. Instead he favored hard-nosed interpretations, such as behavioral and object relations based theories, because they have more the feeling of science to them. Granted that empiricism has a hard edge to it, and that those theories that deflate human pretensions and confound common sense notions have a special place in scientific investigation, one wonders here whether, in the consistent preference for the hard-nosed interpretations, Becker was not himself demonstrating how deeply he had imbibed at the spring of the fictitious heroism of the scientific self-image.

I suggest that Martin Buber's existential philosophy of I-It and I-Thou relationships carries all of the empirical phenomenological and scientific value of behavioral and object relations theories and can be placed on equal scientific footing with these theories. Yet in Buber's I-Thou relationship of genuine mutuality, we find at least an opening that makes theoretically possible the kind of relationships that human beings regularly report in their experience and that they seem to most value (Friedman 1992). This is not to say that an alternative approach such as Buber's makes it easy to attain the I-Thou relationship of mutuality and intimacy. Buber also saw that the objectified I-It relationship is the normal relationship, the relationship toward which even I-Thou relationships tend if such are not consciously fostered and tended. The I-Thou relationship actually has an ideal-typical character. But by at least describing the contours of the genuine and mutual relationship, the Buberian perspective, as a possibility, does not cut it off at the knees. It proceeds in the recognition that a genuine, intimate, and mutual relationship cannot be described exhaustively in behavioral terms, which corresponds to the most deeply felt experience of real human beings.

The psychological and pastoral counselor may well want to explore in therapy those relationships of clients that most approximate the I-Thou relationship. In so doing they might help the client toward fostering and strengthening such relationships. I have found that fostering and tending such relationships have been integral to my own spiritual and personal growth. Such relationships are authentic and valued intimations of transcendence.

Compassionate Extentions of Self in Others

Another side effect of the object relations approach is to refer everything back to the self as an issue of self-knowledge. Again, as a tool for understanding personal motivations, this can be valuable. However, living as we do in what Christopher Lasch (1979) has called the "culture of narcissism," such primary reference to the self needs to be supplemented by other perspectives if it is to be kept from degenerating into a simple ideological support for standardized cultural heroics. The blind spots of this approach are made most clear when it comes to motivations of compassion and altruism. Of course much that goes on in this society under the name of compassion, altruism, and philanthropy is little more than socially sanctioned modes of self-aggrandizement for the socially privileged. But again, I don't think that this tells the story exhaustively.

Journalist Michael Ventura recently wrote about a feeling of genuine compassion (*mitleid,* which means suffering with) when he encountered a homeless man approximately his own age. When he brought this up in a therapy session, the therapist proceeded to explore with him only the "selfish" nature of his reaching out in compassion to this homeless man (Hillman and Ventura 1992). There is nothing wrong with exploring the self in relation to human feelings of compassion. But a theory that makes this the first line of inquiry and exploration in therapy, tending to deflate the compassionate gesture, and that rarely gets beyond that level, needs studied supplementation. No one, and certainly not Becker, is expecting the therapist to simply function as a cheerleader for the noble side of human nature. Yet an approach that only deflates and devalues such gestures is also less than helpful. Compassionate extensions of the self in the community of people, when pursued in balance with other forces and motivations, can be encouraged in actions and explored in therapy as a vehicle for spiritual and psychological growth. Human beings are animals, to be sure, but "animal" does not mean only selfish and vicious! (Kohn 1990). Such compassionate gestures are real and genuine. They are an intimation of transcendence.

Stages of Grief

Kübler-Ross (1969) outlined five basic stages in the process of dying patients in learning about and facing their terminal condition: denial, anger, bargaining, depression, and acceptance. More recently these stages have been built upon by grief counselors James and Cherry (1988) in helping clients to move beyond loss. James and Cherry outlined these stages as gaining awareness, accepting responsibility, identifying recovery communications, taking actions, and finally moving beyond loss.

One of the things that Becker's work gives us is a deep understanding of the fact that the loss of almost any object, if it has been invested symbolically with transference power, can be experienced by the person as a mortal loss. The person may well have the same sorts of blockage, depression, and impediments to the forward movement of living as a terminal patient confronting his or her condition, or of a person grieving the loss of a close family member or friend.

This suggests the possibility that a therapy beyond

Becker would do well to pay close attention to the explorations and ideas emerging from grief therapy and experimentally apply these to situations of loss in which organismic death plays no direct role. This might be efficacious because it treats these losses on a psychological level for what they really are. By accompanying the client through the stages of grieving in relation to these intermediate experiences of loss/death, it might also be possible to assist the client toward awareness of actual death anxiety and in claiming this death awareness as an ally in life. This might be one route into the depths of spiritual and psychological growth that would otherwise be overlooked.

The Human Experience of Love

Becker also wrote rapturously about love as that which transcends the body/spirit dualism of human experience. He wrote movingly on love in a number of places, referring to love as a "primary need" (1964b, p. 141), as the ideal and goal of "aesthetic longing" (1964b, p. 241), as the one "counter-fictional" element in life (1964b, p. 250), as that which "enriches the world" (1968b, p. 186), as the source of human liberation (1968b), and as the "highest way" (1973, p. 233). But because Becker is so fully emersed in the psychoanalytic tradition's bent to distrust positive emotions, his overall account strongly suggests that while the negative emotions are real and basic, the positive emotions are more likely to be tainted and ambivalent, defense techniques, or at best, ideal-typical, that is, less than fully real. Although I would suggest no drawing back from the hard-nosed investigation of the ambivalent nature of our positive emotions, and no slighting of confrontation with the shadow side of our emotional life, I think that finally we learn to trust the authenticity of our positive emotions as well as our negative emotions.

While Becker unquestionably experienced the merger of deep love for his wife, child, and others, he often seemed stranded by his transactional and object relations frame of reference from giving the human experience of love its full due and recognition. He seemed stranded by the fact that the empirical method does not fully recognize love in its own right, but tends to see it primarily as a narcissistic defense. There are many motivations for love, and much that is called love in our lives is hardly worthy of the word. Hard-nosed recognition of this fact is integral to spiritual and psychological growth. Yet once again, while acknowledging fully the gain in viewing this noble human emotion from the behavioral and empirical perspective, we finally have to question whether a perspective that only deflates and devalues what so many human beings assert has been most significant and meaningful in their lives is not in need of studious supplementation.

Psychiatrist Willard Gaylin (1986) has suggested that "certain subjects must be experienced as well as analyzed to be understood; the emotions are a prime example" (p. 6). All of what was written above on the I-Thou relationship could be brought into consideration here, pointing toward love as the paradigm emotional motivation for and fruit of such relationships. I further suggest that the very dynamic of striving for heroism that Becker wrote so much about might, in fact, be a consolation for the lack of having been able to give and to receive real and genuine love in one's life.

The experience of deep caring in love is a fusing experience, an experience in which we catch a glimpse of the unity of body and spirit, which is the goal of therapy and personal growth. This calms the frantic need for heroic achievement to justify one's existence. Exploring the experience of true love is an invaluable ally in helping us to break down dualistic barriers. It helps us to shed those layers of character armor that restrict us and keep us protected, but alone and isolated.

Love is a primary human emotion. Though it can be deformed by the fear of life and the fear of death, it remains a clear intimation of transcendence—an invaluable and indispensable pathway into the discovery of a more perfect balance of these existential pulls, which is the goal of spiritual and psychological growth.

Symbolic Immortality

Becker wrote of immortality striving as the very source of human evil. Without negating a word of what Becker had to say on the subject, I finally must tend toward the view of Robert J. Lifton (1979), who in a truly astonishing work on death and the continuity of life distinguished between healthy and unhealthy immortality striving. Lifton introduced the concept of symbolic immortality thusly: "While I cannot imagine my nonexistence, I can very well imagine a world in which 'I' do not exist. That imaginative capacity is the basis for our theory of symbolic immortality" (p. 8). In direct encounter with Becker's work on the denial of death, Lifton wrote, "While the denial of death is universal, the inner life-experience of a sense of immortality, rather than reflecting such denial, may well be the most authentic psychological alternative to that denial" (p. 13).

Lifton outlined five basic levels of symbolic immortality, each of which can be either healthy or unhealthy in the lives of people:

1. The biological mode, "epitomized by family continuity, living on through, psychologically speak-

ing, in one's sons and daughters and their sons and daughters, with imagery of an endless chain of biological attachment" (p. 18).

2. The theological or religious mode, which "may include a specific concept of life after death" (p. 20).

3. The creative mode, experienced "through great works of art, literature, or science, or through more humble influences on people around us" (p. 21).

4. The mode of nature itself, "the perception that the natural environment around us, limitless in space and time, will remain" (p. 22).

5. The mode of experiential transcendence, a psychic state "so intense and all-encompassing that time and death disappear. This state is the classical mode of the mystic" (p. 24).

These modes of symbolic immortality may be explored in therapy as antidotes to naked death anxiety. It needs to be remembered that there are healthy and unhealthy forms of each of these modes. Each mode can facilitate a life of love, compassion, and psychological and spiritual growth; each mode can function as an immortality ideology that allows the person to continue in a life of compulsive denial. The psychotherapist or counselor must use a pragmatic approach, one that examines relationships and personal behavior, in discerning the degree to which these modes of symbolic immortality are functioning in the life of the client.

While each of these modes of symbolic immortality can be fruitfully explored in psychological and pastoral counseling as an antidote to overwhelming death anxiety, I am most attracted to the practicality of the biological mode. This is a symbol of immortality that is quickly and easily grasped. Of course, the unhealthy varieties of making one's children the symbols of one's own immortality are clearly encountered every day. The violence inherent in working one's own frustrations out on one's family is the motor of most concrete evil we see in our society. Even in a relatively benign form, this unhealthy application of the biological symbol of immortality can place an overwhelming burden of expectations for achievement, and guilt for failure to achieve, on the next generation.

What I find especially attractive in this mode of symbolic immortality is the possibilities it contains for motivating more environmentally responsible behavior in the present. From the sense of symbolic immortality in one's own family, it is not too giant a step to move toward achieving a sense of immortality in the species. At that point, motivation for behavior that is responsible, as the Native American tradition as well as the biblical tradition says, "to the seventh generation," is at least a thinkable counterforce to the current cultural heroics of insatiable grasping, regardless of the environmental destruction that results. To live and act in such a way that one feels personally responsible to the coming generations as the symbol of one's own immortality is a concept that can make sense in our current circumstances.

Much of the curb to the greedy acquisitive material excesses of the post-war period, which hit a sort of high point (low point?) in the 1980s, has been the realization that we are placing intolerable economic and ecological burdens on our grandchildren and great-grandchildren. Certainly this motivation for more environmentally responsible lifestyles is less than what might be hoped for by an idealistic utopian. Yet this has led to measured behavioral changes, at least on the personal level, such as cooperation with recycling programs. This suggests the presence here of fertile material which could be encouraged and reflected upon in psychological and pastoral counseling as an alternative antidote to naked death anxiety.

Loneliness as an Intimation of Transcendence

Shortly before his death, Becker (1974c) penned an article of unusual depth on the subject of loneliness. I consider this article to be a classic in the psychology of spirituality.

Becker begins his exploration by looking at life on this planet, plant life as well as animal life. Most forms of life thrive best in the company of their own kind. Especially in herd and pack animals, Becker saw an emotion akin to loneliness when an individual animal is separated from others. Yet it would be clearly anthropomorphic to describe in animals this intense longing for the company of others in identical terms to that of human beings. The human longing for others and the human experience of loneliness is unique. In animals, the longing for the herd or pack is an instinctual longing, a longing on which the animal is not able to reflect. In human beings, this longing and loneliness spring from a rich interior life that we cannot assume other species share. Only the human being must ask, "What does it mean to inhabit a body? to have been created? what am I doing on this planet? Man is placed in the peculiar position of having to make connection with his own inner self" (Becker 1974c, p. 238). These are questions that cannot be fully answered in relation to the phenomenal world. We look to others for our confirmation of self-worth and self-value. But other human beings cannot give fully satisfactory responses to these questions. No matter how settled one might be in terms of the body, of family and friends, of occupation or career, these questions point one toward a "beyond" for fully satisfactory answers. This is clearly an intimation of transcendence, for as Becker saw, "Loneliness, as dependency on the other, is built into man" (p. 239).

Each human being is a unique individual with a unique interior life. While we are able to open windows to others on this unique interiority in very intimate relationships, the full experience of each individual's interiority is finally closed to all but the personself. This is fundamental to the human experience of loneliness. The human experience of loneliness is a complex emotion. Becker outlined various aspects of being human that contribute to this built-in sense of longing and loneliness.

> Loneliness is built into the human condition in several ways. By dependency on the other, on a "beyond" for validating who one is. By natural narcissism and organismic separateness. By uniqueness of each socialization and the peculiar needs and anxieties it engenders. And finally, by the paradox of Eros vs. Agape strivings, the urge toward both sameness and differences. In sum, there can be no "cure" for a problem that goes this deep into the human condition. [Becker 1974c, p. 241]

Becker spoke of seven gradations of human loneliness. The first of these he called developmental loneliness. This is the loneliness of childhood, in which the child separates itself from objects of its environment in order to come to a better understanding of the self. A second gradation is neurotic loneliness. This is the intense longing of that person who has become so dependent on one object for self-validation that the person is literally lost without it.

Maturational loncliness is the loneliness of the adolescent or young adult who is yet seeking a course in life, a personal identity. A fourth gradation of loneliness Becker called socio-environmental loneliness. This type of loneliness, a result of extreme atomization and destruction of traditional communities and extended families in late capitalism, is made particularly intense in postmodern society. It is that sense of rootlessness that accompanies extreme mobility and individualism. It is the emotional expression of what sociologists have called *anomie.*

Becker also recognized a loneliness of psychosis. This is the loneliness of that person who is denied all agapic sense of belonging, who has developed only very weak techniques of ego defense, who is left feeling exposed and unprotected in the face of the real terror of living. This is the opposite of neurotic loneliness. Closely related to this is what Becker called historical-political loneliness. This is the loneliness of the leader who, as a transference object, has assumed the burden of meaning for large groups of people.

Finally, Becker (1974c) wrote of the loneliness of individuation. This type of loneliness is "the loneliness that is achieved, that is the fruit of a full life, the mark of a mature personality" (p. 244). What Becker was pointing toward in this gradation of loneliness is the idea that even for a person who has accomplished his or her goals in life, who has been confirmed and recognized by others, and enjoys a solid sense of the symbolic immortality, the person must confront the question of the meaning of it all. Because this final question cannot be answered in terms of this world alone, because this final question forces one toward a "beyond," it is a clear intimation of transcendence.

On the other hand, in the postmodern world we get no

unambiguously convincing answers from the beyond toward which we yearn. Our experience of God is for the
most part a fragmented encounter with disenchantment,
absence, and silence. A mature and wise loneliness, an
emotion of continued longing, is finally the best that
this-worldly human existence can offer. In the face of this
reality, a seasoned resignation, a willingness to live with
the longing and loneliness in hope rather than to seek a
cure, is the concluding wisdom of being human. Becker
suggested that this kind of mature loneliness, of mature
wisdom, is most often first achieved in old age.

In the course of his professional writing, Becker finally
looked toward a grounded, solid, reasoned, and freely
chosen religious faith as the concluding answer to the
human dilemma, as the final answer to spiritual, psychological, and personal growth. He maintained in his work an
ongoing dialogue between social science, psychology, and
theology. In his mature work, he achieved what he considered to be a closure of social science and psychology on the
religious faith represented by Kierkegaard and Paul Tillich.

I have found in Becker's work a significant and essential contribution to psychological and pastoral counseling.
Becker's work reminds us that regardless of the progress
we have made, we remain in a state of continuing need. His
work brings closure of the goals of counseling and personal
growth on the deep spirituality represented in the re-
nowned prayer of Reinhold Niebuhr (1976), which has
been adapted by the recovery movement as the Serenity
Prayer:

Oh God!

That transcendent beyond to which I must finally address
my life; that transference object, that source of power

that does not aggress against my full individuality because it is the source of my individuality.

> Grant me the courage to change those things that I can change!

Lead me beyond encumbering constrictions imposed on me, both internally and externally, by my socialization process, which are causing myself and others real pain, which blunt my sense of exhilaration and marvel in the face of life's possibilities because I cannot see the fictitious nature of these constrictions.

> To accept those things which I cannot change!

Knowing that human existence is limited by many forces, whose final symbol is death, do not let me give in to despair, but let me enjoy the truly good things, the gifts of love and relationship, the wonder and amazement of being, which living offers.

> And give me the wisdom to know the difference!

Do not let me become complacent through denial and repression, but lead me into that habit of living which is a mature and wise sense of loneliness, my longing for merger with You.

References

Becker, E. (1961a). *Zen: A Rational Critique*. New York: W. W. Norton.

_____ (1961b). Private versus public logic: some anthropological notes on the problem of mental health. *American Journal of Psychiatry* 118:205–211.

_____ (1962a). Anthropological notes on the concept of aggression. *Psychiatry* 25:327–338.

_____ (1962b). Toward a comprehensive theory of depression. *Journal of Nervous and Mental Disease* 135: 26–35.

_____ (1962c). Towards a theory of schizophrenia. *Archives of General Psychiatry* 7:170–181.

_____ (1962d). Socialization, command of performance, and mental illness. *American Journal of Sociology* 67: 494–501.

_____ (1962e). *The Birth and Death of Meaning: A Perspective in Psychiatry and Anthropology*. New York: Free Press.

_____ (1963). Personality development in the modern world: beyond Freud and Marx. In *Education and the Development of Nations*, ed. H. W. Burns, pp. 83–105. Syracuse, NY: Syracuse University Press.

_____ (1964a). Mills' social psychology and the great historical convergence on the problem of alienation. In *The New Sociology: Essays on Social Theory and Social Values in Honor of C. Wright Mills*, ed. I. Horowitz, pp. 108–133. New York: Oxford University Press.

_____ (1946b). *The Revolution in Psychiatry: The New Understanding of Man.* New York: Free Press.

_____ (1967). *Beyond Alienation: A Philosophy of Education for the Crisis of Democracy.* New York: George Braziller.

_____ (1968a). The second great step in human evolution. *Christian Century*, January 31, pp. 135–139.

_____ (1968b). *The Structure of Evil: An Essay on the Unification of the Science of Man.* New York: Free Press.

_____ (1969). *Angel in Armor: A Post-Freudian Perspective on the Nature of Man.* New York: Free Press.

_____ (1971). *The Lost Science of Man.* New York: George Braziller.

_____ (1972). *The Birth and Death of Meaning: An Interdisciplinary Perspective on the Problem of Man*, 2nd ed. New York: Free Press.

_____ (1973). *The Denial of Death.* New York: Free Press.

_____ (1974a). A conversation with Ernest Becker. *Psychology Today* April:71–80.

_____ (1974b). An anti-idealist statement on communication. *Communication* 1:121–127.

_____ (1974c). The spectrum of loneliness. *Humanitas* 10:237–246.

_____ (1975). *Escape from Evil*. New York: Free Press.

_____ (1977). Letters from Ernest. *Christian Century*, March 9, pp. 217–227.

_____ (1990). The self as a locus of linguistic causality. In *Life as Theater: A Dramaturgical Sourcebook*, ed. D. Brissett and C. Edgley, pp. 117–128. New York: de Gruyter.

Beers, W. (1992). *Women and Sacrifice: Male Narcissism and the Psychology of Religion*. Detroit: Wayne State University Press.

Brown, N. O. (1959). *Life Against Death*. Middletown, CT: Wesleyan University Press.

Carus, P. (1969). *The History of the Devil and the Idea of Evil*. New York: Bell.

Forde, G. (1982). *Justification by Faith—A Matter of Death and Life*. Philadelphia: Fortress.

Freud, S. (1921). Group psychology and the analysis of the ego. *Standard Edition* 18.

_____ (1930). Civilization and its discontents. *Standard Edition* 21.

Friedman, M. (1992). *Religion and Psychology: A Dialogical Approach*. New York: Paragon House.

Gaylin, W. (1986). *Rediscovering Love*. New York: Viking Penguin.

Gergen, K. (1990). Toward a postmodern psychology. *Humanistic Psychologist* 18:23–34.

Giovacchini, P. (1987). *A Narrative Textbook of Psychoanalysis*. Northvale, NJ: Jason Aronson.

Goffman, E. (1959). *The Presentation of Self in Everyday Life*. New York: Anchor-Doubleday.

Goldstein, H. (1990a). The knowledge base of social work practice: theory, wisdom, analogue, or art? *Families in Society* 71:32–43.

_____ (1990b). Strength or pathology. Ethical and rhetorical contrasts in approaches to practice. *Families in Society* 71:267–275.

Gorman, J. (1993). Postmodernism and the conduct of inquiry in social work. *Affilia: The Journal of Women and Social Work* 8:247–264.

Gottwald, N. (1979). *The Tribes of Yahweh.* Maryknoll, NY: Orbis.

Harkness, G. (1945). *The Dark Night of the Soul: From Spiritual Depression to Inner Renewal.* Nashville, TN: Abingdon.

Hartman, A. (1991). Words create worlds. *Social Work* 36:275-276.

Hillman, J. (1985). *Archetypal Psychology: A Brief Account.* Dallas: Spring.

Hillman, J., and Ventura, M. (1992). *We've Had a Hundred Years of Psychotherapy: And the World's Getting Worse.* San Francisco: HarperCollins.

Hopcke, R. (1989). *A Guided Tour of the Collected Works of C. G. Jung.* Boston: Shambhala.

Jager, B. (1991). Psychology in a postmodern era. *Journal of Phenomenological Psychology* 22:60–71.

James, J., and Cherry, F. (1988). *The Grief Recovery Handbook.* New York: Harper and Row.

Keen, S. (1974) A day of loving combat. *Psychology Today* April:71.

Kitwood, T. (1990). Psychotherapy, postmodernism, and morality. *Journal of Moral Education* 19:3–13.

Kluckhohn, F. (1950). Dominant and substitute profiles of cultural orientations: their significance for the analysis of social stratification. *Social Forces* 28:376–386.

Kohn, A. (1990). *The Brighter Side of Human Nature: Altruism and Empathy in Everyday Life.* New York: Basic Books.

Kübler-Ross, E. (1969). *On Death and Dying.* New York: Macmillan.

Kvale, S. (1990). Postmodern psychology: A contradictio in adjecto? *Humanistic Psychologist* 18:35–54.

Kyle, R. (1993). *The Religious Fringe: A History of Alternative Religions in America.* Downers Grove, IL: InterVarsity.

Laplanche, J., and Pontalis, J.-B. (1973). *The Language of Psycho-analysis.* New York: W. W. Norton.

Lasch, C. (1979). *The Culture of Narcissism: American Life in an Age of Diminishing Expectations.* New York: Warner.

Leifer, R. (1976). Becker, Ernest. In *The Encyclopedia of the Social Sciences,* vol. 18, pp. 44–49. New York: Macmillan/Free Press.

Liechty, D. (1990). *Theology in Postliberal Perspective.* Philadelphia: Trinity Press International.

Lifton, R. J. (1979). *The Broken Connection: On Death and the Continuity of Life.* New York: Simon and Schuster.

Lyotard, J. (1984). *The Postmodern Condition: A Report on Knowledge.* Minneapolis: University of Minnesota Press.

Mailick, M. (1991). Re-assessing assessment in clinical social work practice. *Smith College Studies in Social Work* 62:3–19.

Marks, S. J. (1991). *Something Grazes Our Hair: Poems by S. J. Marks.* Urbana: University of Illinois Press.

Meyer, J. (1975). *Death and Neurosis.* New York: International Universities Press.

Moody, R. (1975). *Life after Life.* Covington, KY: Mockingbird Books.

–––––– (1977). *Reflections on Life after Life.* Covington, KY: Mockingbird Books.

Niebuhr, R. (1976). *Justice and Mercy.* New York: Harper and Row.

Rabinow, P., and Sullivan, W. (1987). The interpretive

turn: a second look. In *Interpretive Social Science: A Second Look*, ed. P. Rabinow and W. Sullivan, pp. 1–30. Berkeley: University of California Press.

Rank, O. (1958). *Beyond Psychology*. New York: Dover.

_____ (1968). *Art and Artist: Creative Urge and Personality Development*. New York: Agathon.

Reich, W. (1970). *The Mass Psychology of Fascism*. New York: Simon and Schuster.

Roffey, A. (1993). Existentialism in a post-modern world: meaningful lessons for the counselor. *Counseling and Values* 37:129–148.

Rorty, R. (1979). *Philosophy and the Mirror of Nature*. Princeton: Princeton University Press.

Saleeby, D. (1988). *Theory and the Generation and Subversion of Knowledge*. Lawrence, KS: School of Social Work, University of Kansas.

_____ (1994). Culture, theory and narrative: the intersection of meanings in practice. *Social Work* 39:351–359.

Sartre, J.-P. (1956). *Being and Nothingness*. New York: Philosophical Library.

Schwartz, S. (1986). *Classic Studies in Psychology*. Mountain View, CA: Mayfield.

Shotter, J. (1990). Getting in touch: the metamethodology of a postmodern science of mental life. *Humanistic Psychologist* 18:7–22.

Szasz, T. (1961). *The Myth of Mental Illness: Foundations of a Theory of Personal Conduct*. New York: Harper.

Wilken, R. (1984). *The Christians as the Romans Saw Them*. New Haven: Yale University Press.

Yalom, I. (1980). *Existential Psychotherapy*. New York: Basic Books.

Publications of Ernest Becker

Becker, E. (1960). Psychotherapeutic observations on the Zen discipline. *Psychologia* 3:100–112.

_____ (1961). A note on the primal horde theory. *Psychoanalytic Quarterly* 30:413–419.

_____ (1961). Private versus public logic: some anthropological notes on the problem of mental health. *American Journal of Psychiatry* 118:205–211.

_____ (1961). The psychotherapeutic meaning of east and west. *American Imago* 18:3–20.

_____ (1961). *Zen: A Rational Critique*. New York: W. W. Norton.

_____ (1962). Anthropological notes on the concept of aggression. *Psychiatry* 25:327–338.

_____ (1962). Toward a comprehensive theory of depression. *Journal of Nervous and Mental Disease* 135:26–35.

_____ (1962). Towards a theory of schizophrenia. *Archives of General Psychiatry* 7:170–181.

_____ (1962). Socialization, command of performance, and mental illness. *American Journal of Sociology* 67:494–501.

_____ (1962). The relevance to psychiatry of recent research in anthropology. *American Journal of Psychotherapy* 16:660–617.

_____ (1962). *The Birth and Death of Meaning: A Perspective in Psychiatry and Anthropology.* New York: Free Press.

_____ (1963). Personality development in the modern world: beyond Freud and Marx. In *Education and the Development of Nations,* ed. H. W. Burns, pp. 83–105. Syracuse, NY: Syracuse University Press.

_____ (1963). The significance of Freudian psychology. *Main Currents* 19:45–50, 61–66.

_____ (1964). Mills' social psychology and the great historical convergence on the problem of alienation. In *The New Sociology: Essays on Social Theory and Social Values in Honor of C. Wright Mills,* ed. I. Horowitz, pp. 108–133. New York: Oxford University Press.

_____ (1964). *The Revolution in Psychiatry: The New Understanding of Man.* New York: Free Press.

_____ (1967). *Beyond Alienation: A Philosophy of Education for the Crisis of Democracy.* New York: George Braziller.

_____ (1968). The second great step in human evolution. *Christian Century,* January 31, pp. 135–139.

_____ (1968). *The Structure of Evil: An Essay on the Unification of the Science of Man.* New York: Free Press.

_____ (1969). *Angel in Armor: A Post-Freudian Perspective on the Nature of Man.* New York: Free Press.

_____ (1971). *The Lost Science of Man*. New York: George Braziller.

_____ (1972). The spirit and the ghosts of sociology. *Indian Journal of Sociology* 3:79–82.

_____ (1972). *The Birth and Death of Meaning: An Interdisciplinary Perspective on the Problem of Man*, 2nd ed. New York: Free Press.

_____ (1973). *The Denial of Death*. New York: Free Press.

_____ (1974). A conversation with Ernest Becker. *Psychology Today* April:71–80.

_____ (1974). An anti-idealist statement on communication. *Communication* 1:121–127.

_____ (1974). The spectrum of loneliness. *Humanitas* 10:237–246.

_____ (1974). Toward the merger of animal and human studies. *Philosophy of the Social Sciences* 4:235–254.

_____ (1975). *Escape from Evil*. New York: Free Press.

_____ (1977). Letters from Ernest. *Christian Century*, March 9, pp. 217–227.

_____ (1982). Growing up rugged: Fritz Perls and gestalt therapy. *ReVision* 5:6–14.

_____ (1990). The self as a locus of linguistic causality. In *Life as Theater: A Dramaturgical Sourcebook*, ed. D. Brissett and C. Edgley, pp. 117–128. New York: de Gruyter.

Works of Related Interest

Aden, L. (1984). The challenge of Becker: a new approach to pastoral care. *Journal of Psychology and Christianity* 3:74–79.

Arcaro, T., and Cox, T. (1988). Human existence as a waltz of eros and thanatos. *Humanity and Society* 12:75–94.

Bakan, D. (1966). *The Duality of Human Existence.* Chicago: Rand McNally.

Baumeister, R. (1991). *Escaping the Self.* New York: Basic Books.

Benson, J. (1986). Ernest Becker: A new enlightenment view of evil? *Dialog* 25:101–107.

Bianchi, E. (1977). Death and transcendence in Ernest Becker. *Religion in Life* 46:460–475.

Bregman, L. (1984). Three psycho-mythologies of death: Becker, Hillman and Lifton. *Journal of the American Academy of Religion* 52:461–479.

_____ (1992). *Death in the Midst of Life; Perspectives on Death from Christianity and Depth Psychology.* Grand Rapids. MI: Baker Book House.

Choron, J. (1963). *Death and Western Thought.* London: Collier Macmillan.

Cohen, I. (1982). *Ideology and Unconsciousness.* New York: New York University Press.

Evans, D. (1979). The denial of death. *Religious Studies Review* 5:25–34.

Feifel, H., ed. (1959). *The Meaning of Death.* New York: McGraw-Hill.

_____ (1977). *New Meanings of Death.* New York: McGraw-Hill.

Firestone, R., and Catlett, J. (1989). *Psychological Defenses in Everyday Life.* New York: Human Sciences.

Fleischman, P. (1990). *The Healing Spirit: Explorations in Religion and Psychotherapy.* New York: Paragon House.

Frankl, V. (1969). *The Will to Meaning.* New York: New American Library.

Friedman, M. (1982). *The Human Way.* Chambersburg, PA: Anima Books.

Fromm, E. (1963). *The Dogma of Christ and Other Essays on Religion, Psychology and Culture.* New York: Holt, Rinehart and Winston.

_____ (1973). *The Anatomy of Human Destructiveness.* New York: Holt, Rinehart and Winston.

Gerkin, C. (1979). *Crisis Experience in Modern Life: Theory and Theology for Pastoral Care.* Nashville, TN: Abingdon.

Hartz, G. (1980). The denial of death: foundations for an integration of psychological and theological views of personality. *Journal of Psychology and Theology* 8:53–63.

Hocking, W. (1957). *The Meaning of Immortality in Human Experience.* New York: Harper and Brothers.

Homans, P. (1989). *The Ability to Mourn: Disillusionment and the Social Originis of Psychoanalysis.* Chicago: University of Chicago Press.

Jacobs, H. (1981). Ernest Becker: a reconsideration. *Humanity and Society* 5:239–245.

Jones, J. (1991). *Contemporary Psychoanalysis and Religion: Transference and Transcendence.* New Haven: Yale University Press.

Karpf, F. (1976). More about Becker. *Journal of the Otto Rank Association* 2:26–30.

Kastenbaum, R. (1993). Reconstructing death in postmodern society. *Omega: The Journal of Death and Dying* 27:75–89.

Kaufman, G. (1993). *In Face of Mystery: A Constructive Theology.* Cambridge: Harvard University Press.

Kenel, S. (1988). *Mortal Gods: Ernest Becker and Fundamental Theology.* Lanham, MD: University Press of America.

Killilea, A. (1980/81). Death consciousness and social consciousness. *Omega* 11:185–200.

Kluckhohn, C. (1949). *Mirror for Man: A Survey of Human Behavior and Social Attitudes.* Greenwich, CT: Fawcett.

Kopas, J. (1982). Becker's anthropology: the shape of finitude. *Horizons* 9:23–36.

Kopp, S. (1978). *An End to Innocence: Facing Life Without Illusions.* New York: Macmillan.

Kurtz, E., and Ketcham, K. (1992). *The Spirituality of Imperfection: Modern Wisdom from Classic Stories.* New York: Bantam.

Laughlin, H. P. (1979). *The Ego and Its Defenses.* New York: Jason Aronson.

Lifton, R. J. (1987). *The Future of Immortality.* New York: Basic Books.

———— (1993). *The Protean Self: Human Resilience in an Age of Fragmentation.* New York: Basic Books.

May, R. (1967). *Psychology and the Human Dilemma.* Princeton, NJ: D. Van Nostrand.

May, R., et al. (1958). *Existence: A New Dimension in Psychiatry and Psychology.* New York: Basic Books.

McCarthy, E. (1981). The sources of human destructiveness: Ernest Becker's theory of human nature. *Thought* 56:44–57.

McDargh, J. (1983). *Psychoanalytic Object Relations Theory and the Study of Religion: On Faith and the Imaging of God.* Lanham, MD: University Press of America.

Milgram, S. (1974). *Obedience to Authority.* New York: Harper and Row.

Mowrey, M. (1992). Dualism and the dialectic: a reconsideration of the problem of evil in the work of Ernest Becker. (Unpublished).

Progoff, I. (1956). *The Death and Rebirth of Psychology.* New York: Julian.

Rank, O. (1950). *Psychology and the Soul.* New York: A. S. Barnes.

Richer, P. (1990). Psychological interpretation: a deconstructionist view. *Humanistic Psychologist* 18: 55–63.

Sanford, J. (1981). *Evil: The Shadow Side of Reality.* New York: Crossroad.

Scimecca, J. (1978). The educational theory of Ernest Becker. *Journal of Educational Thought* 12:100–107.

———— (1979). Cultural hero systems and religious beliefs: the ideal-real social science of Ernest Becker. *Review of Religious Research* 21:70–72.

Schneider, K. (1990). *The Paradoxical Self: Toward an Understanding of Our Contradictory Nature.* New York: Plenum.

Sontag, F. (1981). Anthropodicy or theodicy? A discussion with Becker's *The Structure of Evil. Journal of the American Academy of Religion* 49:267–274.

Staub, E. (1989). *The Roots of Evil: The Origins of Genocide and Other Group Violence.* Cambridge: Cambridge University Press.

Stroebe, M., Gergen, M., Gergen, K., and Stroebe, W. (1992). Broken hearts or broken bonds: love and death in historical perspective. *American Psychologist* 47:1205–1212.

Thompson, R. (1975). *Psychology and Culture.* Dubuque, IA: Wm. C. Brown.

Toulmin, S. (1986). Self psychology as a "postmodern" science. *Psychoanalytic Inquiry* 6:459–477.

Westphal, M. (1984). *God, Guilt, and Death: An Existential Phenomenology of Religion.* Bloomington: Indiana University Press.

White, D., and Hellerich, G. (1992). Postmodern reflections on modern psychiatry. *Humanistic Psychologist* 20:75–91.

Index